# How to
# Live a Good Life

# How to
# Live a Good Life
*following* NEW TESTAMENT *ethics*

Václav Rajlich

TAN Books
Charlotte, North Carolina

Printed With Ecclesiastical Permission.
Most Reverend Earl Boyea. July 4, 2018

ISBN: 978-1-5051-1361-7

Library of Congress Control Number: 2018948052

Published in the United States by
TAN Books
PO Box 410487
Charlotte, NC 28241
www.TANBooks.com

Printed in the United States of America

# Table of Contents

# 1
## *Introduction*

In the late 1970s, my youngest brother John lived in a modest house in a Prague suburb, with a small group of fellow former students who secretly joined the Dominican order. To be a Dominican was illegal in Communist Czechoslovakia and carried a stiff jail sentence. A police raid could have occurred at any time.

Visiting John one day, he introduced me to his friends. We sat down in their living room, drank coffee, and chatted about their studies and jobs. Then one of them asked, "Do you want to meet Pavel?" The question surprised me, but I said, "Sure."

Through a narrow hallway, they led me to the back room where Pavel was lying in bed; he was less than thirty years old, about the same age as my brother. As I walked in, Pavel turned his head and smiled. John introduced me and Pavel told me that he had heard of me and prayed for me and my loved ones. Not a single word was said about Pavel or his suffering.

I thanked him for his prayers. As I was leaving the room, he waved; this small gesture required great effort. Back in the living room, I asked: "Who is Pavel?" They told me that he was their friend, who had metastatic cancer, and that he was in constant terrible pain. Even though his pain was so bad, he was sent home from the hospital and was waiting for either a miracle or death.

Traveling home through the darkened streets of Prague in a streetcar, I was thinking about Pavel Legerský and how he radiated inner peace, undiminished by his life of pain, or fear of a possible police raid that could take away his caretakers. That sharply contrasted with my own restlessness and anxiety, in spite of my much more comfortable circumstances. I was wondering whether I would ever achieve that peace of mind.

This book summarizes what I have learned since my brief encounter with Pavel. It begins with a short overview of the academic discipline of ethics.

## 1.1 Ethics

During our lives, we perform numerous *human acts*; some are voluntary, others are involuntary. Every *voluntary human act* involves a deliberate *choice* and employs both human reason and will. In this book, the word "act" will mean "voluntary human act". *Ethics* or *moral philosophy* is an academic discipline that studies voluntary acts and the choices that lead to them. It also answers the questions: "What is the right act in these circumstances?" and "What is the best way to live?"

Many people believe that ethics is a simple topic and does not need much attention. They think that it is sufficient to follow what they learned early in their life, or to copy the prevailing mores of their environment. However, they overlook how many ethical traps are set for the unwary. While they may hire a mechanic to fix their car because it is too complex, they believe that their own unsophisticated ethics will be enough to help them to successfully navigate the ethical shoals and rocks they encounter in their lives.

The people who understand the need to study ethics are immediately confronted by a bewildering array of teachers with widely divergent and contradictory recommendations. Some of these teachers have influenced entire societies. An incomplete list includes Confucius, Buddha, Mohammed, Plato, Kant, and Marx.

When dealing with these ethical systems, we should remember the New Testament warning: "...Can a blind man lead a blind man? Will they not both fall into a pit?" (Lk 6:39). Some dangers are not immediately apparent:

> *"Beware of false prophets, who come to you in sheep's clothing but inwardly are ravenous wolves. You will know them by their fruits. Are grapes gathered from thorns, or figs from thistles? So, every sound tree bears good fruit, but the bad tree bears evil fruit. A sound tree cannot bear evil fruit, nor can a bad tree bear good fruit. Every tree that does not bear good fruit is cut down and thrown into the fire. Thus you will know them by their fruits." (Mt 7:15-20)*

## 1.2 Pursuing Big Goals

In the face of a wide difference of advice within disparate ethical systems, the pursuit of big goals provides a helpful metaphor. Big goals require sustained effort and offer great rewards. For example, an entrepreneur starts a new high tech company that becomes profitable after years of hard work. A mother sacrifices years of her life and brings up a child to a productive adulthood. A neighbor plants vegetables in the spring, tends them through the summer, and harvests them in the fall. They all know that pursuing big goals brings rewards and satisfaction. Deep in our hearts, we too long for the rewards that only big goals can bring.

The opposite is aimlessness, living for the moment, drifting through life. There is nothing attractive about it. It is a symptom of an unsatisfactory life.

Many teachers, preachers and mentors know that and they advise their charges to "think big." They encourage children to have "big dreams" because they know that the pursuit of big goals is an indispensable part of human flourishing. Pagan Romans summarized it in a proverb *"Per aspera ad astra,"* that is, "A rough road leads to the stars." Big goals are illustrated by the following examples.

**Hannah's Road Trip to Chicago**

Hannah has a friend in Chicago who invited her for a weekend visit. She has accepted the invitation and drives from Detroit. Before and during her trip, she considers her options. She is faced with some choices that are good, others that are not so good. Her decisions should follow *rules* (or *precepts* or *commandments* or *principles* or *practices*) that can be structured into *four pillars (4Ps)*:

1. *Prohibited Acts:*
   Do not drive on the left side of the road; you will not get very far if you do that. Also do not drink and drive.

2. *Prescriptions:*
   Double-check your friend's address and make sure it is correct. Get enough gas, or stop for gas when the gas tank is getting low.

3. *Priorities:*
   Since your goal is to visit a friend in Chicago, do not leave Detroit and drive, say, in the opposite direction over the Ambassador Bridge to Canada. However, on your trip to Chicago, you can stop for a snack or for a swim in Lake Michigan at the Warren Dunes. But if you do, make sure that you get back on the road on time.

4. *Providence:*
   Be mindful that there are things beyond your control which can turn your Chicago trip either into a success or a failure. You hope that there will be no accidents either on the road or while swimming in the lake. In case you have an unexpected car breakdown, you hope that there will be a towing service and a nearby repair shop that can fix your car.

There are also choices that do not impact the success of Hannah's goal. It does not matter whether she drives a red or a blue car, whether she packs sandwiches or eats at a fast food restaurant, or, if she takes the toll road, whether she pays using cash or a credit card. Some choices are *significant* for achieving her big goal and should follow the principles in the four pillars above, while others are *insignificant* and subject to personal preference.

Her reward of the successful trip to Chicago is an enjoyable weekend in the Windy City, in the company of her friend.

Hannah's road trip to Chicago is an example of a journey. People often compare the pursuit of a big goal to a journey. Many see themselves as travelers or pilgrims.

## Jacob's Study for a Bachelor's Degree

Another familiar example of a big goal is learning. It takes years to earn a bachelor's degree, for example in computer science. During those years, Jacob contemplates various choices and is advised to follow the ensuing principles:

1. *Prohibited Acts:*
   Do not cheat on exams! You can be expelled from school for cheating.

2. *Prescriptions:*
   Be diligent, study hard, keep up with the lecture material, do the homework.

3. *Priorities:*
   Do not take too many courses that do not contribute to earning your degree. Remember, your goal is to get the bachelor's degree in computer science. However you may take several interesting electives outside of your major. Also, it helps to avoid parties the night before your finals, although you can relax and socialize during the semester.

4. *Providence:*
   Hope that you will have good health, the talent, and the finances required to complete the studies.

The reward of Jacob's studies is the new knowledge and a bachelor's degree, which will open the door to a fulfilling career. People often

. _ the pursuit of a big goal to learning and see themselves as students, disciples, or apprentices.

## 1.3 The Biggest Goal in Life

As important as other big goals are, one specific big goal towers over all others: We want to experience our whole life as a success rather than as a futility and failure. We will attain that success if we follow Jesus of Nazareth. He taught how to reach the *Kingdom of God* that offers peace of mind during our life and eternal happiness afterwards.

The relevant passage in the New Testament is: "Peace I leave with you; my peace I give to you. Not as the world gives do I give to you. Let not your hearts be troubled, neither let them be afraid" (Jn 16:33). This highly desirable goal eludes many of our contemporaries who frantically search for it, but Pavel Legerský attained it in his dire circumstances by following Jesus of Nazareth.

The eternal happiness after death is promised in this passage: "... no eye has seen, nor ear heard, nor the heart of man conceived, what God has prepared for those who love Him" (1 Cor 2:9).

All other big goals pale in comparison. The New Testament makes that very clear with the following words of caution: "For what does it profit a man, to gain the whole world and forfeit his life?" (Mk 8:36, Lk 9:25, Mt 16:26).

Jesus taught us how to pursue this biggest goal of our life. His teachings apply to all circumstances, including the most challenging ones, like the ones in which Pavel Legerský found himself. In this book, I call this teaching *New Testament Ethics*.

> ▪ **Interpreting New Testament**
>
> Ethical teachings are intertwined throughout the New Testament with other topics, such as historical narrative, theology, ecclesiology, and prophecies. Some teachings are encoded in parables and need decoding, while others are tersely expressed and thus need unpacking. Some teachings are gathered from events, as Jesus not only taught by

his words but also by his actions. Also, some of the other persons in the New Testament offer examples worthy of emulation, while others display a behavior that serves as a warning.

The teachings have to be explained because they may be hard to understand. Jesus himself said "…they may indeed see but not perceive, and may indeed hear but not understand…" (Mk 4:12). The phrases "not understand" or "not yet understand" are often repeated in the New Testament, giving a hint of the difficulty readers might experience (Jn 3:7, Lk 2:50, Mk 4:12, Mt 13:19).

An honest interpretation of the Bible is called *exegesis*. Reading into that text whatever we want to hear is *eisegesis*. As a warning, the New Testament contains an example of eisegesis by an ill-willed interpreter: The devil quotes scriptures in support of his temptation of Jesus (Mt 4:5-7).

While understanding the New Testament may be a challenge, it is not hopeless. The Gospels explain:"…I thank thee, Father, Lord of heaven and earth, that thou hast hidden these things from the wise and understanding and revealed them to babes"(Mt 11:25).

We want honest advice on how to reach the Kingdom of God. That means that we want exegesis. The Church is a great help for this task. She has pondered every sentence of the New Testament through two thousand years and has provided numerous resources to help us.

## Story of the Rich Young Man

The story of the rich young man is an abbreviated version of the entire New Testament Ethics, a kind of executive summary:

*And behold, one came up to him, saying, "Teacher, what good deed must I do, to have eternal life?" And he said to him, "Why do you ask me about what is good? One there is who is good. If you would enter life, keep the commandments." He said to him, "Which?" And Jesus said, "You shall not kill, You shall not commit adultery, You shall not steal, You shall not bear false witness, Honor your father and mother, and, You shall love your neighbor as yourself."*

> *The young man said to him, "All these I have observed; what do I still lack?" Jesus said to him, "If you would be perfect, go, sell what you possess and give to the poor, and you will have treasure in heaven; and come, follow me." When the young man heard this he went away sorrowful; for he had great possessions.*
>
> *And Jesus said to his disciples, "Truly, I say to you, it will be hard for a rich man to enter the kingdom of heaven. Again I tell you, it is easier for a camel to go through the eye of a needle than for a rich man to enter the kingdom of God." When the disciples heard this they were greatly astonished, saying, "Who then can be saved?" But Jesus looked at them and said to them, "With men this is impossible, but with God all things are possible." (Mt 19:16–26)*

In the beginning of this story, the rich young man encounters Jesus. He is already convinced about the value of pursuing life's biggest goal (the rich young man calls it "eternal life"), and asks Jesus of Nazareth how to achieve it (Mt 19:16). In the first reply, Jesus indicates that only God determines what is good and therefore leads to the Kingdom of God (Mt 19:17). It is the human role to learn what that path is, not to invent it. After this introduction, there is a very brief summary of the four pillars of the New Testament ethics (4Ps) that lead to the Kingdom of God:

1. *Prohibited Acts:*
   You shall not kill. You shall not commit adultery. You shall not steal. You shall not bear false witness (Mt 19:19).

2. *Prescriptions:*
   Honor your father and mother. You shall love your neighbor as yourself (Mt 19:20).

3. *Priorities:*
   Jesus said to him, "If you would be perfect . . . come, follow me" (Mt 19:21).

*4. Providence and Grace:*
With men this is impossible, but with God all things are possible (Mt 19:26).

While a small part of Jesus' advice applies specifically to the rich young man (first part of Mt 19:21), the rest is addressed to all of us, whether rich or poor, young or old, man or woman. Other parts of the New Testament contain numerous clarifications of these short answers. We must note, however, that reaching the Kingdom of God requires more than what is required for an earthly success. That is further discussed in Chapter 5.

I hope and pray that the reader follows the example of Pavel Legerský and accepts the advice of Jesus, unlike the rich young man who walked away sorrowful.

## 1.4 Further Study

Thomas Aquinas studied the pursuit of big goals and called them "arduous good", see Part 2, Q. 18 (Aquinas, 1948).

The *Catechism of Catholic Church* explains the full extent of God's Word that consists of the Old Testament, New Testament, and sacred tradition (CCC 50–141). This book relies mostly on a subset recorded in the New Testament.

There are numerous publications that present the ethical teachings of the New Testament. Pope Benedict XVI (2007) presents a scholarly overview of the life and teachings of Jesus of Nazareth. While some theologians focus on the differences in the perspective among the New Testament authors, Schnackenburg (1965) highlights important unifying themes, although, on page 12, he incorrectly complains that "Jesus did not elaborate a system of moral theology."

Veritatis Splendor points to the story of the rich young man as the key to understanding the ethical system of the New Testament (VS 6–27). This idea is the organizing principle of this book. Ratzinger (2005) discusses the potential impact of Veritatis Splendor on the discipline of moral theology.

The Ten Commandments, also called the Decalogue, is a time tested summary of biblical prescriptions. The Decalogue is based on two texts of the Old Testament (Exodus 20:1-17, Deuteronomy 5:4-21). Table 1.1 classifies the commandments according to the pillar they belong to.

Human acts are the basic component of human behavior and as such, they are the center of attention of ethics and other academic disciplines. *Psychology* studies human perceptions, emotions, motivations, will, reason, habits, and so forth; all these aspects of human personality have an impact on human acts. *Psychiatry* deals with mental disorders that may also impact human act.

Table 1.1 The Ten Commandments and the Four Pillars

| Commandments | Pillar |
|---|---|
| 1 (partially), 2, 5, 6, 7, 8, 9, 10 | Prohibited acts |
| 3, 4 | Prescriptions |
| 1 | Priorities |

Pinckaers (2001) summarizes the historical development of the Catholic moral teachings.

MacIntyre (1984) describes the contemporary fragmentation of ethics and the possible social consequences.

**Questions for Reflection or Group Discussion**

1.  What is ethics in general, and the New Testament Ethics in particular?

2.  Is the New Testament easy to understand?

3.  Is it necessary to learn from the Church's understanding of the New Testament?

4.  Present some examples of four pillar reasoning as it relates to big goals.

5.    Invent your own examples of a big goal and the relevant four pillars.

## References

Aquinas, T. (1948). *Summa Theologica*. New York: Benziger Bros.

Benedict, XVI. (2007). *Jesus of Nazareth: From the Baptism in the Jordan to the Transfiguration*. New York: Doubleday.

MacIntyre, A. (1984). *After virtue*. Notre Dame: University of Notre Dame.

Pinckaers, S. (2001). *Morality: The Catholic View*. South Bend: St. Augustine's Press.

Ratzinger, J. (2005). *The Renewal of Moral Theology: Perspectives of Vatican II and Veritatis Splendor*. Communio, 32(2), 357.

Schnackenburg, R. (1965). *The Moral Teaching of the New Testament*. New York: Herder and Herder.

# 2
# *Prohibited Acts*

Following the order Jesus used in the dialog with the rich young man, we begin our exposition of New Testament Ethics with a brief overview of prohibited acts (Mt 19:16–26).

Obviously, not everything we can do should be done, such as the example noted in the previous chapter about driving a car on a freeway in the wrong direction. Although we can do it, it is an invitation to disaster. The same can be said about attempts to get an academic degree by cheating.

Prohibitions are rules that keep us on the right track on our path towards big goals. Prohibitions are conceptually very simple; so simple that small children can understand and learn them. The first ethical lessons that a small child encounters are prohibitions: "Do not touch the hot stove!" and "Do not throw your food on the floor!"

## 2.1 The New Testament Prohibitions

The New Testament prohibitions rule out grossly immoral interactions with other people. Adherence to them allows us to seek the Kingdom of God, the same way adherence to traffic rules allows Hannah to travel to Chicago or adherence to university rules allows Jacob to study for a degree. The prohibitions listed in the New Testament are few and brief (Mt 19:19), but Jesus applies them broadly.

The New Testament prohibitions can be compared to a dangerous precipice. It is prudent to keep a safe distance from the edge, not to test how closely we can get before we fall off. Unfortunately, some visitors underestimate this danger at such locations as the Grand Canyon, and fatal accidents happen ("Man falls to his death at Grand Canyon," 2014).

## You Shall Not Kill

This prohibition is the foundation of civilized life. Whenever societies have not respected this prohibition, the life of their communities has been crippled by fear. Jesus expands this commandment and prohibits any injury to any human being, whether it is a bodily injury or a psychological one:

> *"You have heard that it was said to the men of old, 'You shall not kill; and whoever kills shall be liable to judgment. But I say to you that every one who is angry with his brother shall be liable to judgment; whoever insults his brother shall be liable to the council, and whoever says, 'You fool!' shall be liable to the hell of fire." (Mt 5:21-22)*

## You Shall Not Commit Adultery

Jesus prohibits any sexual acts except those acts between a husband and wife within a lifelong marriage that are open to life. The prohibition applies even to thoughts and actions done in private: "You have heard that it was said, 'You shall not commit adultery.' But I say to you that every one who looks at a woman lustfully has already committed adultery with her in his heart" (Mt 5:27-28).

But why are New Testament teachings on sexuality so strict? Sexuality is closely tied to human life; a new life starts with sexual union. This new life deserves protection from the very beginning and that can be guaranteed only if the life begins in orderly circumstances. A cavalier attitude towards sex inevitably leads to a cavalier attitude towards human life.

Sexual drive is indeed one of the most powerful natural human instincts. Many advertisers, peddlers of titillating "art," or outright pornographers, know how to exploit sexuality and turn it into profit. If unchecked, sexual drive can turn our earthly life into a wreck and block us from reaching the Kingdom of God.

This prohibition often leads into a difficult battle during one's teenage years and continues throughout one's whole adult life. There are many exhortations in the New Testament that remind us of this battle, for example: "Do you not know that your body is a temple of the Holy Spirit within you, which you have from God? You are not your own; you were bought with a price. So glorify God in your body" (1 Cor 6:19-20).

Unnatural sexual acts are grave offenses that are specifically prohibited in several passages of the New Testament:

> *For this reason God gave them up to dishonorable passions. Their women exchanged natural relations for unnatural, and the men likewise gave up natural relations with women and were consumed with passion for one another, men committing shameless acts with men and receiving in their own persons the due penalty for their error. (Rom 1:26-27; see also 1 Cor 6:10, 1 Tim 1:10)*

## You Shall Not Steal

This prohibition requires respect for the property of others. Societies that do not or cannot protect property experience chaos and poverty. St. Paul implores thieves to change their ways (Eph 4:28).

## You Shall Not Bear False Witness

Witnesses testify in court and their testimony serves to convict or acquit defendants. In other contexts, witnesses observe important events like weddings or contract closings and testify about the validity of these acts. Being a false witness can seriously harm other people.

Jesus applies a broad interpretation of this commandment and disallows all lying, i.e., any intentionally misleading statement. He counsels great caution with the spoken word: "I tell you, on the day of judgment men will render account for every careless word they utter; for by your words you will be justified, and by your words you will be condemned" (Mt 12:35-37).

Lying can be addictive because it offers an easy escape out of unpleasant situations. Like all addictions, it tends to grow from seemingly innocent lies to serious ones.

Because of the many forms of lies and their seductive nature, telling the truth has to be constantly practiced, even in small things. The truth needs to be stated with brevity and directness, without evasion: "Let what you say be simply 'Yes' or 'No'; anything more than this comes from evil" (Mt 5:37).

Note that big goals cannot be reached without truth. For a successful journey, travelers need to know the sometimes uncomfortable truth about where they are—or aren't—and which direction they need to take to get to their desired destination. Our journey towards the Kingdom of God needs the same level of honesty.

Often there are competing opinions and confusing explanations of the facts around us (Jn 18:38), and speaking and otherwise living the truth gives us experience that helps us to decipher these situations. As Jesus confirms: "[A]nd you will know the truth, and the truth will make you free" (Jn 8:32).

In some circumstances, telling the truth may involve danger. Jesus gives an example how to respond in such situations:

> One day, as he was teaching the people in the temple and preaching the gospel, the chief priests and the scribes with the elders came up and said to him, "Tell us by what authority you do these things, or who it is that gave you this authority." He answered them, "I also will ask you a question; now tell me, Was the baptism of John from heaven or from men?" And they discussed it

*with one another, saying, "If we say, 'From heaven,' he will say, 'Why did you not believe him?' But if we say, 'From men,' all the people will stone us; for they are convinced that John was a prophet." So they answered that they did not know whence it was. And Jesus said to them, "Neither will I tell you by what authority I do these things." (Lk 20:1-7)*

This Gospel story presents a pattern how to refuse an answer to somebody who does not deserve the truth. Instead of answering the question, Jesus asked a counter-question and after an unsatisfactory and calculated reply, he also refused to answer. He certainly did not get out of this tight spot by a lie. This is an example for us how to handle similar difficult situations, not by lie, but insisting on our right to remain silent. Likewise, we are fully entitled to put the questioners on the spot, to prompt them to reveal any embarrassing motivation. We are permitted to withhold the truth from those who do not deserve it. But we are not permitted to lie.

Lying dulls our moral compass and therefore it is a dead end on our way through life. It is not a coincidence that evil systems like Nazism and Communism were based on lies. Lying allows covering up crimes that could not survive the glare of truth. Lying is often the first indication that something is wrong with a person or with a society. Lying is a gateway to other sins. Where lying abounds, theft, sexual immorality, and murder, are not far behind.

> **▪ How truth can be twisted**
>
> Eskimos live in constant contact with snow and they have developed about 50 different words for various forms of it (Robson, 2013). We live in an environment saturated by lies and therefore it is no surprise that we also have developed many different expressions for various types of lies. The list below is an incomplete classification of lies and their different levels of gravity:
>
> • *False witness* is the original content of the commandment and it is a lie about a significant event. Depending on the gravity of the matter, it may be a serious crime.

- *Perjury* is lying under oath; it is an aggravated instance of false witness.

- *Euphemism* is a substitution of unpalatable truth by a better sounding statement. "Pregnancy interruption" is one of the most infamous euphemisms; it is a misnomer for the murder of the pre-born child.

- *Spin* is a testimony twisted to the speaker's own advantage, often through euphemisms, omission of pertinent facts, or addition of irrelevant facts. The presenter paints a picture structured in such a way that it is likely to mislead the listener.

- *Disinformation* is professionally produced spin that targets large populations.

- *Noble lie* is meant to accomplish good. In the mind of the liar, the listeners are not ready for the harsh truth or would interpret it in a wrong way. Therefore, the noble lie is used for their good.

- *White lie* is a small deception that does not seem to hurt anybody (or so we think): "Tell the caller that I am not here." A special subcategory of white lies we tell to our innocent children, for example, Santa Claus brings Christmas presents; the stork delivers babies. These are widespread and have a poetic component. Nevertheless, there is a potential for harm. The children, once they learn the truth, may grow up skeptical about other parental testimonies and may consider lying to be a normal part of life.

- *Glamorous lie* is so creative that it succeeds in its purpose and against all odds. It is sometimes celebrated in books and movies as an admirable skill.

- *Calumny* attacks somebody's reputation.

- *Coercive lie* is extracted from the victim by force, torture, or a threat.

- *Bullying lie* is intended to intimidate. There is something scary about brazen liars and a person understandably asks, "If they can get away with this, what else can they do to me?"

- *Beyond the pale* means something unacceptable. In a well-ordered society, "within the pale" is equal to truth and "beyond the pale" is a lie. Unfortunately however, this often is not the case. Then we have four possible combinations. First, truth within the pale is the domain of decent people. Second, truth beyond the pale is the domain of heroes. Jesus and his followers often found themselves in this position. Third, lying within the pale is the domain of careerists and opportunists. Fourth, lying beyond the pale is the domain of scoundrels.

- *Pathological liar* is a person who considers lying to be a right and, instead of being embarrassed, gets angry when caught.

- *Denial* is a willful wrong belief that a victim holds, even though all evidence is to the contrary. It is usually driven by the fear of unpleasant truth.

- *Sucker (dupe)* is a person willing to accept a lie. A sucker does not seek the truth but clings to a comfortable lie.

## 2.2 Sin

Violations of the New Testament prohibitions are called *sins. Mortal sin* is the conscious and voluntary transgression in grave matter. It totally sabotages the goals of reaching the Kingdom of God and the consequences are severe. Because of the serious nature of mortal sins, the New Testament counsels avoiding them under any circumstances and at any personal cost. The New Testament contains harsh language in describing sin: "He who commits sin is of the devil; for the devil has sinned from the beginning…" (1 Jn 3:8). In Chapter 5, we will return to the topic of sin in the context of God's mercy.

However, we all know that not all transgressions are equal. Some are very serious, others are minor and they present a lesser threat to the goal of reaching the Kingdom of God. These lesser transgressions are called *venial sins*. In the analogy of Hannah's road trip to Chicago, minor traffic violations, such as slightly exceeding the speed limit, present an increased risk of an accident and may result in a traffic ticket, though they still allow her to continue driving to Chicago.

In our battle against sin, our "heart," that is, the core of our being from which our choices originate, is the first battlefield. Our thoughts, dreams, fantasies, plans, and attitudes, sooner or later result in outward deeds: "For from within, out of the heart of man, come evil thoughts, fornication, theft, murder, adultery, coveting, wickedness, deceit, licentiousness, envy, slander, pride, foolishness. All these evil things come from within, and they defile a man" (Mk 7:21-23).

It is very important for us to wage this battle of the heart. It is a lifelong battle that is never fully won, but we must never concede defeat. Jesus rebuked the scribes and Pharisees who misunderstood this connection and concentrated only on visible acts. He likened them to "whited sepulchres . . . full of all filthiness" (Mt 23:27).

*Coveting* is a desire of things that are not ours or that are not good for us. It is an Old Testament prohibition that, if unheeded, can play havoc with our destiny. The warning against it is repeated in the New Testament: "You desire and do not have; so you kill. And you covet and cannot obtain; so you fight and wage war . . ." (Jas 4:2).

## 2.3 Legalism and its Limits

Prohibitions are one of the pillars of the New Testament Ethics, but some ethicists created simplistic ethical systems where prohibitions became the only ethical principle, the only pillar on which their ethical systems rest. These are called *legalistic systems.* In these systems, prohibitions are complemented by legal duties which compel certain actions. These legal duties can be understood as prohibitions against inaction in certain situations.

One characteristic feature of the legalistic systems, which separates them from the New Testament, is the attempt to define precise boundaries between what is prohibited and what is permitted. Note that the New Testament uses a broad interpretation of the prohibitions and, as a consequence, the boundaries between prohibited and permitted are somewhat vague. Legalistic systems, however, try to have boundaries that are very sharp and precisely defined.

These sharp boundaries invite a fallacy that considers everything that is legal to be also moral. The fallacy provides a convenient excuse that "the act was legal," even if it is obviously wrong. Experience shows that there are many ways in which it is possible to wrong someone by perfectly legal means.

The legalistic systems also encourage people to ask: How far can I go without violating the prohibition? This approach is called "finding loopholes" and it is one of the dark sides of legalistic systems. Legalists, in response, try to close these loopholes through various contingencies and stipulations. They also wage an unending tug-of-war against the smart and creative loophole seekers. This leads to an explosion in the number and complexity of laws. It also causes trivialization of the law where the heavy-handed apparatus of law is used in trivial situations that need a lesser remedy.

The New Testament presents the Pharisees as examples of legalism. The Pharisees tried to construct the entire ethical system as a system of prohibitions (or legal duties) and ended up with a hugely complex system. Some of their prohibitions, particularly prohibitions against activities on the Sabbath, lacked common sense. More on that is in Chapter 6.

*Legalistic Christianity* is a simplistic ethical system that tries to reduce the New Testament Ethics to prohibitions or legal duties. Adherents of such a system do not understand that there are multiple pillars of New Testament morality, but try to reduce everything to one pillar. Their simplistic system is a throwback to the mindset of the Pharisees.

On several occasions, Jesus found himself in conflict with artificial prohibitions of Pharisees. There is a seeming paradox where Jesus on one hand counsels very strict observance of some laws (Mt 5:21-22), but on the other hand advocates a very loose approach to other laws (Lk 6:6-11). The solution of this paradox is in differentiation of the four pillars of the New Testament Ethics. True prohibitions have to be observed very meticulously, while correct reasoning about the other three pillars follows a different pattern and is discussed in the ensuing chapters.

## 2.4 Further Study

New Testament prohibitions are traditionally presented as a part of the Ten Commandments (CCC 2258–2557, VS 12-13). The Catechism of Catholic Church discusses mortal and venial sin, including grave acts that are done without complete consent or full knowledge (CCC 1849–1864).

Natural law is a unified theory that guides reasoning about the prohibitions. A summary of natural law can be found in several publications, including May & Hickey (1994) and Finnis (2011).

## Questions for Reflection or Group Discussion

1.  List contemporary offenses against the prohibition "You shall not kill" that society tolerates.

2.  How is the commandment "You shall not commit adultery" applied in the New Testament?

3.  What is wrong with white lies? Noble lies?

4.  Is the observance of prohibitions sufficient to reach the Kingdom of God?

## References

Finnis, J. (2011). *Natural law and natural rights*: Oxford University Press.

May, W. E., & Hickey, J. A. (1994). *An introduction to moral theology*: Our Sunday Visitor.

Robson, D. (2013). *There really are 50 Eskimo words for 'snow'*. http://www.washingtonpost.com/national/health-science/there-really-are-50-eskimo-words-for-snow/2013/01/14/e0e3f4e0-59a0-11e2-beee-6e38f5215402_story.html (3/19/2016)

*Texas man falls 350 feet to his death at Grand Canyon.* (2014). http://www.cbsnews.com/news/texas-man-falls-350-feet-to-his-death-at-grand-canyon/ (3/19/2016)

# 3
# *Prescriptions*

Hannah knows that following traffic rules alone is not enough to reach Chicago, because there are challenges on the road. She must buy gas before her gas tank is empty, watch other cars on the road, and more. Jacob knows that in order to earn a bachelor's degree, it is not sufficient to follow the university rules, he also must choose courses wisely and to study hard.

Similarly, more than just keeping prohibitions is needed to reach the Kingdom of God. In this chapter, we present the prescriptions that comprise the second pillar of the New Testament Ethics. They tell us how to deal with some of the challenges that we may encounter.

## 3.1 Virtuous Acts

Dealing with challenges requires an effort. A *deficiency* means the effort is inadequate, while an *excess* is an overreaction. In contrast, a *virtuous act* is the optimal effort. That optimum is also called "balance," "the sweet spot" or "the golden mean," and it lies somewhere between deficiency and excess. *Aristotelian analysis* explains not only the sought optimum, but also the whole range of options that include both the deficiency and excess, and the process of how to achieve the optimum (Aristotle). In this chapter, we use *virtue* to mean virtuous acts, while a failure to act virtuously, either by a deficiency or excess, is called *vice*.

Many technical problems are solved by finding the optimum. Suppose that we want to set a temperature in a living room in winter. The deficiency is the room that is too cold (not enough heat), the excess is a room that is too hot (too much heat), and the optimal temperature is in between. To set the right room temperature, we have to know both the current and the optimal room temperature. If there is a deviation, we have to take corrective action: Increase the heating if the room is too cold, or decrease the heating if the room is too hot. A thoughtless increase of heating, no matter how hot or cold the room is, is not a solution, but rather leads to a vice of excess, as we end up with an overheated room. Similar reasoning applies when seeking virtues.

This chapter discusses the most important virtues that are necessary for a successful journey towards the Kingdom of God; additional virtues appear in the Appendix.


## 3.2 Rationality

Reason is one of the great gifts that we possess and we must use it, whenever we encounter problems in our pursuit of the goals. New Testament authors make constant appeal to our reason and rightly so. They want us to think about the way we act. Correct reasoning about acts is called *rationality*; synonyms or closely related notions are "prudence," "forethought," "wisdom," "common sense," and "good judgment." A rational act requires the following steps:

1. Get all available and relevant facts.

2. Analyze those facts, consider the options and choose the best one.

3. Take action.

The deficiency is often called "irrationality," "rashness," "impulsiveness," "cluelessness," or "foolishness." These words mean that the person does not gather available important facts, nor analyzes them correctly.

The opposite vice is the excess: It can be an unending gathering of facts because something is always missing. It also can be an inability to arrive at a decision. In either case, it leads to a delayed action or no action at all. This vice is called "analysis paralysis," "big design up front," "procrastination," or "stalling." Since all virtues require rationality, it could be called the "mother of all virtues."

## Rationality and Feelings

*Feelings* (or "emotions" or "passions") are inner reactions that prompt us to act in a certain way. There are positive feelings that bring satisfaction and negative feelings that cause discomfort. Rationality requires finding the proper place for them in our decision making.

Basing our acts exclusively on emotions is irrational, as feelings are often blind. The opposite extreme is a complete suppression of feelings and acting in a robot-like manner. Both of these vices represent a serious threat to our goal of reaching the Kingdom of God. Feelings represent an important ingredient in assessing a situation and should therefore be taken into account with appropriate moral weight, which is neither overwhelming, nor negligible.

New Testament exhortations appeal to our reason. They let us know that reason should have a decisive role in the course of our actions. However Jesus also manifested strong feelings, indicating that they also have their place in our decisions. There were flashes of justified anger (Jn 2:15), weeping over the death of Lazarus (Jn 11:35) and fear of approaching danger (Lk 22:44). The following two examples show Jesus acting in the presence of strong feelings. In the first, Jesus is justifiably angry, with both reason and feeling in accord:

> *In the temple he found those who were selling oxen and sheep and pigeons, and the money-changers at their business. And making*

*a whip of cords, he drove them all, with the sheep and oxen, out of the temple; and he poured out the coins of the money-changers and overturned their tables. And he told those who sold the pigeons, "Take these things away; you shall not make my Father's house a house of trade." (Jn 2:14-16; see also Mt 21:12-13, Mk 11:15-17)*

The second example occurred in the Garden of Gethsemane:

*Then Jesus went with them to a place called Gethsemane, and he said to his disciples, "Sit here, while I go yonder and pray." And taking with him Peter and the two sons of Zebedee, he began to be sorrowful and troubled. Then he said to them, "My soul is very sorrowful, even to death; remain here, and watch with me." And going a little farther he fell on his face and prayed, "My Father, if it be possible, let this cup pass from me; nevertheless, not as I will, but as thou wilt."*

*And he came to the disciples and found them sleeping; and he said to Peter, "So, could you not watch with me one hour? Watch and pray that you may not enter into temptation; the spirit indeed is willing, but the flesh is weak." Again, for the second time, he went away and prayed, "My Father, if this cannot pass unless I drink it, thy will be done." And again he came and found them sleeping, for their eyes were heavy. So, leaving them again, he went away and prayed for the third time, saying the same words. Then he came to the disciples and said to them, "Are you still sleeping and taking your rest? Behold, the hour is at hand, and the Son of man is betrayed into the hands of sinners." (Mt 26:36-45, see also Mk 14:32-42)*

In Gethsemane, Jesus was troubled by a strong fear. He did not ignore his fear and sought to alleviate it through praying to his Father and also through the companionship of his disciples. But, in the end, rather than fleeing the danger as urged by his fear, he stayed, was arrested, and underwent his suffering and death.

If our reason, will and feelings work in accord, the act we intend to do is easy. In contrast, when there is a discord between these traits of our personality, the planned act can be difficult. If the feelings are overwhelming, Jesus shows us that the prayer and companionship with friends may help us to cope. In any case, Jesus shows that we should give priority to the use of the reason and thus choose to do the right thing.

## 3.3  Proactive Virtues

Proactive virtues govern acts that we freely undertake, based on our own initiative, when we have wide latitude for action.

### Fortitude

In our lives, we experience inconveniences or difficult situations. There are physical dangers, severe weather, and other perilous situations. There also are social and psychological threats, financial setbacks, employment and family problems, or the fear of the unknown. The problems can be stark or they can be subtle and the stakes can be high or small. In all of these cases, our fears can lead to paralysis, an inability to act.

*Fortitude* frees our will and allows us to do the right thing in the presence of inconvenience, danger, or fear. Fortitude can be further understood through the synonyms "courage," "bravery," "mettle," "backbone," "grit," or "guts."

Aristotelian analysis places fortitude in the sweet spot between two extremes: *Cowardice* is a deficiency where we allow the fear of danger or inconvenience to completely determine our behavior. The other extreme is *recklessness*, in which we disregard the reality of the danger. Fortitude requires rational assessment of true danger and right action in its presence.

Note that experiencing fear is humanly understandable and appropriate when something is truly dangerous, but it is an obstacle when the danger is not serious. Given the circumstances, listening to our fears is sometimes the right thing to do, while sometimes it is not. Exercising fortitude—like all other virtues—relies on rationality to make the distinction.

There are numerous examples of courage in the New Testament. St. Joseph overcame his fear of the unknown and of a potential scandal regarding Mary's pregnancy and took her as his wife (Mt 1:20). Joseph of Arimathea, in spite of his fear of the high priests and the Romans, requested and received the body of Jesus, and gave Jesus a dignified burial (Mk 15:43). St. Paul fearlessly embarked on an apostolic mission to the center of the world power of his time (Acts 23:11).

There can be competition between fears. We can fear a trivial danger but disregard a much more serious one, hence showing cowardice and recklessness at the same time. The all-powerful God certainly should be feared: "I tell you, my friends, do not fear those who kill the body, and after that have nothing more that they can do. But I will warn you whom to fear: fear him who, after he has killed, has authority to cast into hell. Yes, I tell you, fear him!" (Lk 12:4-5).

Every act of courage blazes a trail for others. Heroes who acted courageously in the past, made it easier for us to do the right thing without fear in the present. Through their courage and against great odds, they built the sound foundation on which we now stand.

## Justice and Mercy

Justice and mercy are twin virtues that govern the power of the strong over the weak. This power can be formally defined, such as the power of bosses over employees, parents over children, teachers over students, judges over defendants, or commanders over soldiers. Or it can be informal such as the power of the physically strong over the physically weak, the armed over the unarmed, the rich over the poor, or the group over the individual.

In fact, every relationship can involve power as we grant or refuse wishes or make demands. The power presents opportunities to exercise justice and mercy. Justice and mercy are so closely inter-twined that the best approach is to treat them together (James 2:13).

*Merciful justice* is the virtue of a person who, with generosity and benevolence, grants the recipients either what is their due or more. It is the sweet spot between two extremes: The error to one extreme, the deficiency, is an *unjust act* (or *unjust inaction*) that either seriously violates the recipients' rights, or allows them to get away with seri-ous trespasses. The error to the other extreme, the excess, is *severity*, where people are caught in a difficult situation and mercilessly receive their just desert. The biblical parable of the unmerciful servant warns against the excess of severity (Mt 18:23-35).

> *Therefore the kingdom of heaven may be compared to a king who wished to settle accounts with his servants. When he began the reckoning, one was brought to him who owed him ten thousand talents; and as he could not pay, his lord ordered him to be sold, with his wife and children and all that he had, and payment to be made. So the servant fell on his knees, imploring him, 'Lord, have patience with me, and I will pay you everything.' And out of pity for him the lord of that servant released him and forgave him the debt.*
>
> *But that same servant, as he went out, came upon one of his fellow servants who owed him a hundred denarii; and seizing him by the throat he said, 'Pay what you owe.' So his fellow servant fell down and besought him, 'Have patience with me, and I will pay you.' He refused and went and put him in prison till he should pay the debt. When his fellow servants saw what had taken place, they were greatly distressed, and they went and reported to their lord all that had taken place. Then his lord summoned him and said to him, 'You wicked servant! I forgave you all that debt because you besought me; and should not you have had mercy on your fellow servant, as I had mercy on you?' And in anger his lord delivered him to the jailers, till he should pay all his debt. So also my heav-enly Father will do to every one of you, if you do not forgive your brother from your heart. (Mt 18:23–35)*

The first servant had a perfect right within the legal system of the time to do what he did, but he acted without any regard to the plight of his fellow servant. The king reacted strongly by revoking his own mercy towards the merciless servant and treated him with the same severity as that servant showed towards his colleague. The warning of the parable is clear: God deals severely with those who deal harshly with others.

Another New Testament parable illustrates merciful justice in action. This story is often called the "Parable of Prodigal Son," but perhaps a better name would be the "Parable of the Merciful Father," because the father is the true hero of this story and his behavior is the one that we are exhorted to emulate:

*There was a man who had two sons; and the younger of them said to his father, 'Father, give me the share of property that falls to me.' And he divided his living between them. Not many days later, the younger son gathered all he had and took his journey into a far country, and there he squandered his property in loose living. And when he had spent everything, a great famine arose in that country, and he began to be in want. So he went and joined himself to one of the citizens of that country, who sent him into his fields to feed swine. And he would gladly have fed on the pods that the swine ate; and no one gave him anything. But when he came to himself he said, 'How many of my father's hired servants have bread enough and to spare, but I perish here with hunger! I will arise and go to my father, and I will say to him, "Father, I have sinned against heaven and before you; I am no longer worthy to be called your son; treat me as one of your hired servants."' And he arose and came to his father.*

*But while he was yet at a distance, his father saw him and had compassion, and ran and embraced him and kissed him. And the son said to him, 'Father, I have sinned against heaven and before you; I am no longer worthy to be called your son.' But the father said to his servants, 'Bring quickly the best robe, and put it on him; and put a ring on his hand, and shoes on his feet; and bring the fatted calf and kill it, and let us eat and make merry; for this my son was dead, and is alive again; he was lost, and is found.' And they began to make merry.*

*Now his elder son was in the field; and as he came and drew near to the house, he heard music and dancing. And he called one of the servants and asked what this meant. And he said to him, 'Your brother has come, and your father has killed the fatted calf, because he has received him safe and sound.' But he was angry and refused to go in. His father came out and entreated him, but he answered his father, 'Lo, these many years I have served you, and I never disobeyed your command; yet you never gave me a kid, that I might make merry with my friends. But when this son of yours came, who has devoured your living with harlots, you killed for him the fatted calf!' And he said to him, 'Son, you are always with me, and all that is mine is yours. It was fitting to make merry and be glad, for this your brother was dead, and is alive; he was lost, and is found.' (Lk 15:11–32)*

There are three persons in the story — the father, the younger son and the older son. The younger son requests his part of the family inheritance prematurely, before father's death, contrary to all customs and mores. Then he squanders it, ending up destitute. In desperation, he returns home.

If the father in the parable was severe, he would send his wayward son away because the younger son seriously misbehaved, stained the family name, and now would have to face the full consequences. Instead, the father invites the younger son back home, even throwing a party to celebrate his return.

However note that there is no question of dividing the property again. The previous division of the property, which the younger son foolishly requested, cannot be in justice forgotten or undone and all remaining inheritance belongs to the older son (Lk 15:31). The father knows that his *mercy must not cause injustice* and deprive the older son of what is rightfully his. In other words, he does not punish the innocent older son for the misbehavior of the younger one. He knows that to misrepresent mercy towards someone by placing an unjust burden on someone else (older son) is wrong, that in reality, it is a senseless kind of injustice as it punishes the innocent and rewards the guilty.

> **▪ Different, but Consistent Interpretations**
>
> The parable of the prodigal son is often validly used to illustrate God's mercy towards us. In this context, the older son is often presented as somebody who hesitates to accept his father's and, by extension, God's mercy towards his younger brother, thereby showing his own need to grow in virtue.
>
> Our interpretation emphasizes the acts of the merciful father as a human act to emulate. These different interpretations manifest the depth and internal consistency of the New Testament parables: While they often speak of God, they also give us examples to imitate, consistent with an exhortation: "You, therefore, must be perfect, as your heavenly Father is perfect" (Mt 5:48).

The father in this parable found the sweet spot between severity towards younger son and injustice towards older son, and thus serves as an example of merciful justice. The parable of the laborers in the vineyard provides a further clarification of merciful justice:

*For the kingdom of heaven is like a householder who went out early in the morning to hire laborers for his vineyard. After agreeing with the laborers for a denarius a day, he sent them into his vineyard. And going out about the third hour he saw others standing idle in the market place; and to them he said, 'You go into the vineyard too, and whatever is right I will give you.' So they went. Going out again about the sixth hour and the ninth hour, he did the same. And about the eleventh hour he went out and found others standing; and he said to them, 'Why do you stand here idle all day?' They said to him, 'Because no one has hired us.' He said to them, 'You go into the vineyard too.'*

> *And when evening came, the owner of the vineyard said to his steward, 'Call the laborers and pay them their wages, beginning with the last, up to the first.' And when those hired about the eleventh hour came, each of them received a denarius. Now when the first came, they thought they would receive more; but each of them also received a denarius. And on receiving it they grumbled at the householder, saying, 'These last worked only one hour, and you have made them equal to us who have borne the burden of the day and the scorching heat.' But he replied to one of them, 'Friend, I am doing you no wrong; did you not agree with me for a denarius? Take what belongs to you, and go; I choose to give to this last as I give to you. Am I not allowed to do what I choose with what belongs to me? Or do you begrudge my generosity?' (Mt 20:1-15)*

In this story, the householder hired some laborers early in the morning. Out of mercy, he also hired some idle laborers in the late afternoon, knowing that their contribution to the effort would be small. In the evening, the wages were paid and the early morning laborers expected that they would be paid more than those laborers hired later in the day. They were upset when both groups received the same wage.

However note that there was no injustice. The householder paid them their just wage. Their problem was their disapproval of his generosity, combined with envy of the ease with which the late laborers earned their wage. The householder concluded that he had done nothing wrong and persisted with his mercy towards laborers hired late in the day.

The lesson to learn is that although the burden of our mercy must not fall unjustly on innocent people as the previous parable of the merciful father has shown, the other people's disapproval is not a sufficient reason to stop our acts of mercy, as described in the parable of the laborers in the vineyard.

Finally, in yet another Gospel passage Jesus explains that the gifts of wealth, health, and freedom also have to be shared mercifully with our less fortunate neighbors:

*When the Son of man comes in his glory, and all the angels with him, then he will sit on his glorious throne. Before him will be gathered all the nations, and he will separate them one from another as a shepherd separates the sheep from the goats, and he will place the sheep at his right hand, but the goats at the left. Then the King will say to those at his right hand, 'Come, O blessed of my Father, inherit the kingdom prepared for you from the foundation of the world; for I was hungry and you gave me food, I was thirsty and you gave me drink, I was a stranger and you welcomed me, I was naked and you clothed me, I was sick and you visited me, I was in prison and you came to me.'*

*Then the righteous will answer him, 'Lord, when did we see thee hungry and feed thee, or thirsty and give thee drink? And when did we see thee a stranger and welcome thee, or naked and clothe thee? And when did we see thee sick or in prison and visit thee?' And the King will answer them, 'Truly, I say to you, as you did it to one of the least of these my brethren, you did it to me.'*

*Then he will say to those at his left hand, 'Depart from me, you cursed, into the eternal fire prepared for the devil and his angels; for I was hungry and you gave me no food, I was thirsty and you gave me no drink, I was a stranger and you did not welcome me, naked and you did not clothe me, sick and in prison and you did not visit me.' Then they also will answer, 'Lord, when did we see thee hungry or thirsty or a stranger or naked or sick or in prison, and did not minister to thee?' Then he will answer them, 'Truly, I say to you, as you did it not to one of the least of these, you did it not to me.' And they will go away into eternal punishment, but the righteous into eternal life. (Mt 25:31-46)*

This last Gospel passage makes clear that the acts of mercy are absolutely essential on our path towards the Kingdom of God (Mt 25:46). We are asked to show mercy by sharing some of our fortune with those who are less fortunate. Note that the specific acts Jesus mentions are:

- To give food to the hungry
- To give drink to the thirsty
- To welcome the stranger
- To cloth the naked
- To visit the sick
- To visit the prisoners (Mt 25:35-36).

These are the acts required of the seekers of the Kingdom of God who are well-fed, surrounded by friends, clothed, healthy and free. Because mercy is an important virtue, it will be mentioned often in ensuing chapters.


## Love

In our relationships with our neighbors, selfishness creates serious obstacles, but love overcomes that selfishness. Love overlaps with mercy. The difference is that mercy is the attitude of the strong towards the weak, while love can be exercised by all, including the weakest ones. Love goes by synonyms or variants of "charity," "good-will," or "affection."

The New Testament emphasizes love of neighbor as a key virtue and summarizes it in this prescription: "... You shall love your neighbor as yourself" (Mt 22:39 or Lk 10:27). This has been often called "The Golden Rule."

The "Aristotelian middle" is at work in The Golden Rule. Note the connective word: "You shall love your neighbor *as* yourself." The deficiency is *selfishness*, also called "egotism". Selfish people ignore or abuse their neighbor. In contrast, the excess is committed by people who, usually as a coping mechanism in the context of an abuse, have given up on their goals and instead devote their energy to pleasing their neighbor. They erroneously place their neighbor into a position higher than themselves and that position belongs only to God. Various forms of psychological codependency are manifestations of this vice.

Love is often misunderstood. Popular culture tries to reduce it to erotic love and misrepresents it as receiving rather than giving. In this distorted version, even selfish, hurtful and exploitative erotic relations masquerade as "love". Instead, let's pay attention to St. Paul's checklist of true love:

> *Love is patient and kind; love is not jealous or boastful; it is not arrogant or rude. Love does not insist on its own way; it is not irritable or resentful; it does not rejoice at wrong, but rejoices in the right. Love bears all things, believes all things, hopes all things, endures all things. Love never ends. (1 Cor 13:4-8)*

The parable of the Good Samaritan exemplifies great love by someone who follows The Golden Rule:

> *A man was going down from Jerusalem to Jericho, and he fell among robbers, who stripped him and beat him, and departed, leaving him half dead. Now by chance a priest was going down that road; and when he saw him he passed by on the other side. So likewise a Levite, when he came to the place and saw him, passed by on the other side.*
>
> *But a Samaritan, as he journeyed, came to where he was; and when he saw him, he had compassion, and went to him and bound up his wounds, pouring on oil and wine; then he set him on his own beast and brought him to an inn, and took care of him. And the next day he took out two denarii and gave them to the innkeeper, saying, 'Take care of him; and whatever more you spend, I will repay you when I come back.' Which of these three, do you think, proved neighbor to the man who fell among the robbers? He said, "The one who showed mercy on him." And Jesus said to him, "Go and do likewise." (Lk 10:29-37)*

Note that the Good Samaritan does not spare any expense, taking the best possible care of the man victimized by robbers. However he still goes about his business after he leaves the victim in the care of an innkeeper. He does not give up on his goals, but rather continues on with his mission. To completely abandon his goals would be an excess, not the love of the neighbor as himself.

Also note that this parable implies that the victim is a Jew while his rescuer is identified as a Samaritan. In biblical times, Jews and Samaritans were hostile to each other. In spite of that, the Good Samaritan treats the injured Jew with compassion rather than hostility, and this is the behavior that Jesus recommends. By this parable, Jesus teaches that the ethical rules of the New Testament are to be applied in all interactions with all people, not just to our friends or members of our group. In other words, *all people are our neighbors*, even the people who belong to alien or hostile groups. This applies also to unborn children since each unborn child is also part of humanity (Psalm 139:13–16).

## Faith and Trust

Trust is an act of a *trustor* who delegates some responsibility to somebody else, called a *trustee*. In our complex modern society with highly specialized roles, we are regularly in a position of trustors. We are trustors of car mechanics and map makers when traveling by car, trustors of professors when registering and paying for college courses, trustors of pilots when flying in an airplane, trustors of cooks when eating a meal, or trustors of politicians whom we elect to office. The problem that we face is how to handle unreliability in others. There is always a risk that the trustee will betray us, either by negligence or malice.

Trust is the virtue that allows us to handle these ambiguous situations. We evaluate the trustworthiness of trustees based on their reputation, past record, recommendations, and/or certification by professional or regulatory bodies. We reject trustees not worthy of our trust and take a chance on trustees who have been appropriately evaluated. We do not insist on an abstract level of trustworthiness, but accept the reality of the concrete choices before us. Synonyms and variants of the virtue of trust are "belief" and "confidence."

Facing uncertainty related to potential trustees, the trustor must avoid the deficiency of *mistrust*, also called "cynicism," "paranoia," or "unbelief," while not falling into an excess of *gullibility* that puts trust into swindlers. The virtue of trust is the Aristotelian optimum between these two extremes.

*Faith* is a trust in the context of the biggest goal of our life; it is the most important act of trust that we can make. The New Testament presents inspiring examples of faith. One example among many is the centurion, whom Jesus proclaims as a role model to emulate:

> *As he entered Capernaum, a centurion came forward to him, beseeching him and saying, "Lord, my servant is lying paralyzed at home, in terrible distress." And he said to him, "I will come and heal him." But the centurion answered him, "Lord, I am not worthy to have you come under my roof; but only say the word, and my servant will be healed. For I am a man under authority, with soldiers under me; and I say to one, 'Go,' and he goes, and to another, 'Come,' and he comes, and to my slave, 'Do this,' and he does it."*
>
> *When Jesus heard him, he marveled, and said to those who followed him, "Truly, I say to you, not even in Israel have I found such faith. I tell you, many will come from east and west and sit at table with Abraham, Isaac, and Jacob in the kingdom of heaven, while the sons of the kingdom will be thrown into the outer darkness; there men will weep and gnash their teeth." And to the centurion Jesus said, "Go; be it done for you as you have believed." (Mt 8:5-13)*

The New Testament contains other examples of faith (Mt 9:20–22, Mt 9:27-30, Mk 10:52, Mt 7:7, Mt 15:21-28). Jesus chastises some of his listeners for the vice of unbelief:

> *Then he began to upbraid the cities where most of his mighty works had been done, because they did not repent. "Woe to you, Chorazin! woe to you, Beth-saida! for if the mighty works done in you had been done in Tyre and Sidon, they would have repented long ago in sackcloth and ashes. But I tell you, it shall be more tolerable on the day of judgment for Tyre and Sidon than for you.*

*And you, Capernaum, will you be exalted to heaven? You shall be brought down to Hades. For if the mighty works done in you had been done in Sodom, it would have remained until this day. But I tell you that it shall be more tolerable on the day of judgment for the land of Sodom than for you." (Mt 11:20-24)*

Jesus scorns demands for additional proofs, beyond the ones that he has already offered (Mt 12:38-42). He also warns against gullibility and gives a rule to use when assessing the trustee: "Every sound tree bears good fruit, but the bad tree bears evil fruit" (Mt 6:15-20).

## Hope

Reaching any big goal is always uncertain, because unpredictable or unforeseen events can always thwart our pursuit. This uncertainty leads to doubts about the viability and sensibility of the goal. Our doubts increase when we run into difficulties while the goal is still far away. Hope is the virtue that resolves these doubts.

When Hannah travels to Chicago, her hope is the conviction that Chicago can be reached, even when she experiences a car breakdown. When Jacob studies for a bachelor's degree, his hope is the conviction that his studies can be completed, even if he flunks an exam.

Synonyms and variants of hope are "optimism" or "positive thinking." Note that hope deals with things that lie in the future and are uncertain (cf. Rom. 8:24-25, Heb. 11-12). There is no need to practice hope when something is already obvious and assured.

Hope is the Aristotelian middle between two extremes: On one hand, there is the deficiency of *hopelessness*, also called "pessimism," "dejection," or "despair" that impairs or even robs people of their ability to pursue big goals. The excess is *smugness* or *presumption*. A smug person thinks that reaching the big goal is guaranteed, does not take proper precautions, and will be completely thrown off by unanticipated obstacles.

Hope is the sweet spot between these two extremes. While people of hope patiently continue in spite of their doubts, they treat their doubts as useful warnings, and patiently and perseveringly prove them wrong.

Jesus reminds us that the Kingdom of God is difficult to reach (Mt 7:13-14), but hope leads us to believe that we can reach it. Note that no capricious earthly obstacles truly stand in the way; everybody can aspire to reach it. Pavel Legerský, whom I wrote about in the Introduction, was a great example of hope in dire circumstances.

Many people have experienced past perils that they successfully overcame. These successes can serve as an encouragement for our hope. As St. Paul says: "... he delivered us from so deadly a peril, and he will deliver us; on him we have set our hope that he will deliver us again" (2 Cor 1:10).

The virtues of love, faith, and hope are called *theological virtues* and will be further discussed in Chapter 5.

## 3.4 Reactive Virtues

Proactive virtues of the previous section are based on a person's initiative. But initiative is not always ours, as every tennis player or football player knows. Sometimes the circumstances are stronger than we are and we have to react or adapt appropriately. Reactive virtues are virtues for these circumstances. They govern acts that are responses to conditions that cannot (or should not) be ignored.

### Humility

Humility addresses how we perceive ourselves and how we handle that perception. It allows us to see ourselves as we are, without embellishments and without detractions. It is an essential virtue on our path towards all big goals.

There are several synonyms or variants: "self-understanding," "capacity of self-examination," or "sincerity with oneself." Aristotelian analysis places humility into the balance between the following two extremes: One is *hubris*, where human actors greatly overestimate their capabilities and sometimes even think of themselves as equal to

God. Additional synonyms or variants are "pride," "arrogance," "conceit," "haughtiness," "hauteur," "self-importance," and "pomposity." The other extreme is an *inferiority complex* where human actors grossly underestimate or undervalue their capabilities or their standing.

> ▪ **Meaning of the Word "Pride"**
>
> The word "pride" has shifted its meaning in modern culture to a synonym of self-esteem, as in "I am justifiably proud of this achievement." To avoid this unwanted shift in meaning, some writers have resurrected the Greek word "hubris" to describe an unwarranted and destructive exalting of one's own capability or position. But, to be clear, we use word "pride" in this book for the vice, for which "hubris" can serve as a synonym.

An inferiority complex is a doubt about oneself. Note that hubris can co-exist with an inferiority complex. Some people suffer from hubris in one area of their life and an inferiority complex in another. Some people even oscillate from one extreme to the other, never finding the right balance.

The Gospels frequently warn against hubris. Moving away from hubris and closer to humility is called "humbling" oneself; the opposite is called "exalting" oneself: "He who exalts himself will be humbled and he who humbles himself will be exalted" (Mt 23:12; see also Lk 14:11 and Jas 4:10). A popular paraphrase of this New Testament wisdom is: "There are two types of people: Those who are humble and those who are about to be." Jesus presents well-behaved children as an example of humility:

> *At that time the disciples came to Jesus, saying, "Who is the greatest in the kingdom of heaven?" And calling to him a child, he put him in the midst of them, and said, "Truly, I say to you, unless you turn and become like children, you will never enter the kingdom of heaven. Whoever humbles himself like this child, he is the greatest in the kingdom of heaven." (Mt 18:1-4)*

While the New Testament in several passages advises us to humble ourselves, it also encourages us not to fall into an inferiority complex: "But you are a chosen race, a royal priesthood, a holy nation, God's own people, that you may declare the wonderful deeds of him who called you out of darkness into his marvelous light" (1 Pet 2:9). "Know that you are the glory of God" (1 Cor 11:7).

## Moderation

Pleasurable activities provide a rest for a tired traveler, but they can also dissipate our effort and lure us away from our pursuit of our big goals. Moderation or "temperance" addresses how much energy we should allocate to pleasure.

The deficiency is *self-indulgence* or *immoderation*, where the people do whatever their desires dictate, without reasonable limits. Self-indulgence has many specialized names when dealing with different urges: For example, "gluttony" is an immoderate consumption of food and "alcoholism" is an excessive drinking of alcoholic beverages. There are also "compulsive behaviors" like compulsive shopping or compulsive gambling, etc.

The excess is "severity" or "puritanism." Puritans view with suspicion everything that is pleasurable and try to master their urges by complete abstinence from all pleasurable experiences. Moderation is the sweet spot between these two extremes. It allows moderate pleasure, but avoids all excesses that drain energy or resources and thereby undermine or even sabotage our big goals. Synonyms and closely related virtues are "self-control," "self-restraint," "self-discipline," or "temperance."

St. Paul speaks about moderation and draws comparison with the athletes, who also have to demonstrate it: "Every athlete exercises self-control in all things. They do it to receive a perishable wreath, but we an imperishable" (1 Cor 9:25).

The virtues of rationality, fortitude, merciful justice, and moderation are collectively called *cardinal virtues*.

- **Complete Abstinence**

For some desires, complete abstinence is not an excess, but the required virtue. Highly addictive or damaging drugs require complete abstinence. Alcoholics and other addicts also must exercise complete abstinence, because a small indulgence can trigger a restart of the uncontrolled addictive behavior.

## Meekness

Meekness requires making room for others and for God in our life. Synonyms and variants of meekness are "obedience" and "docility." It is different from humility. Humility addresses our self-perception. Meekness addresses our interactions.

Aristotelian analysis places meekness between the following two extremes: The deficiency is *exploitative behavior*, where others are turned into stepping stones that some people use to advance their goals. Variants and synonyms of exploitative behavior are "domineering behavior" or "conceit." The excess is "servility," where the actors allow others to impose their agenda, sometimes even a sinful agenda. Variants and synonyms that can be used to describe servility are "abjectness," "resignation," "ingratiation" or "lack of personality."

Current culture ridicules meekness and considers it to be a trait suitable only for dogs, not for human beings. Despite this scorn, every person who seriously pursues any big goal knows that meekness is an essential virtue. Without it, we face constant strife and are unable to reach our goals. We have to meekly obey traffic rules, follow traffic directions by police, or learn topics taught by the teachers. In sports, the athletes have to follow instructions from coaches. These days, however, to avoid the unpalatable word "meekness," new synonym "coachability" is used.

Jesus recommends meekness in this New Testament passage:

> *You have heard that it was said, 'An eye for an eye and a tooth for a tooth.' But I say to you, Do not resist one who is evil. But if any*

*one strikes you on the right cheek, turn to him the other also; and if any one would sue you and take your coat, let him have your cloak as well; and if any one forces you to go one mile, go with him two miles. Give to him who begs from you, and do not refuse him who would borrow from you. (Mt 5:38-42)*

Elsewhere in New Testament, Jesus gives numerous examples of meek behavior for us to emulate. However he makes clear that meekness cannot be identified with servility and that there is a limit in fulfilling other people's wishes, notably wishes that conflict with our big goals cannot be accommodated:

*And when it was day he departed and went into a lonely place. And the people sought him and came to him, and would have kept him from leaving them; but he said to them, "I must preach the good news of the kingdom of God to the other cities also; for I was sent for this purpose." (Lk 4:42-43)*

## 3.5  More on Reasoning about Prescriptions

In the reasoning about the virtues, we identified virtue as the sweet spot between deficiency and excess. This section refines that and gives warnings about possible errors.

### Intrinsic Evil

In the world, good and evil coexist and are sometimes hard to separate. As a result, many potential deeds involve a mixture of both. *Consequentialism* claims that as long as the result is good, the deed is acceptable, no matter what means are used. This thinking is summarized in the saying, "The end justifies the means." However, St. Paul rejects this thinking: "There are those who say: And why not do evil that good may come? . . . Their condemnation is just" (Rom 3:8).

It is not that hard to see the reason for this rejection. Suppose that instead of being the instigators, we are the recipients. Do we want to be killed, robbed, sexually exploited or lied to, so that somebody can attain some supposed good?

Any act that seriously violates the prohibitions is *intrinsically evil* and cannot be justified by any presumed good that comes from it. When weighing a decision of how to act, the first matter we need to consider is one that explores the moral permissibility of the act. Only when an act is morally permissible can the Aristotelian balancing start.

## Virtues in a Binary World

Some people live in an "either-or" world that offers only two choices for everything: If you reject one choice, you are accepting the other one. Thinking like that is called "binary thinking" or "black and white thinking." It is adequate for the prohibitions described in the previous chapter, but Aristotelian reasoning about virtues does not fit into it and therefore people who are prone to binary thinking have a problem with the full understanding of virtues.

Binary thinking is encouraged by asymmetry in virtues. The Latin maxim states "*in medio stat virtus,*" that is, "virtue lies in the center." However, for some virtues, most people deviate from the virtue in the direction of the deficiency, while the excess is a problem for fewer people. Consequently, preachers and ethicists understandably spend more time talking to people who suffer from deficiencies rather than excesses. The New Testament authors also emphasize that the listeners should extricate themselves from deficiencies and the excesses are sometimes mentioned only very briefly or in a different context.

An example of such asymmetric presentation is the previously noted virtue of meekness that is recommended by a well-known prescription to go an extra mile when forced by anyone to accompany them (Mt 5:41). This prescription is very difficult for many of us, as we are blinded by our selfishness and the false urgency of our petty plans. Therefore, Jesus states this prescription very explicitly so that it gets our attention. However, there is also a previously mentioned and much less-discussed passage in the New Testament, where Jesus rejected people's attempt to keep him from leaving and went on to preach in the synagogues of Judea (Lk 4:42-44). In this event, he exemplified that the excess of servility is to be rejected also.

Moral teachers sometimes fail to warn against excesses. They reason that such warnings may reinforce any deficiencies in their listeners. They may even misrepresent virtues as prohibitions of defects, and end up with a binary system that fits into legalistic Christianity that was mentioned in the previous chapter. However, in order to live a truly moral life, people need to hear the full story, because excesses can be as destructive as deficiencies and the lives of people who are misled by these erroneous teachings can be seriously damaged.

## Anti-legalistic Christianity

*Anti-legalistic Christianity* is an overreaction to legalistic Christianity. It is an ethical system that is based on a single prescription, to "love your neighbor" (Mk 22:39-40). This single prescription implies all prohibitions of the previous chapter, because violations of these prohibitions result in failure to love (Rom 13:9).

While technically correct, there is a problem with the vagueness of the word "love" that may camouflage intrinsic evil. As an example among many, some ethicists defend "mercy killing" as a manifestation of "love," disregarding that it leads directly into the intrinsic evil of killing. In their view, Pavel Legerský whom I mentioned in the introduction, was a prime candidate for mercy killing. We can conclude that only a respect for the explicit biblical prohibitions can bring a necessary clarity into the muddled debate about what is or is not true love.

## Demands on Others

Virtues define how we should behave. However, we can psychologically delude ourselves by turning a virtue on its head, that is, making it into a demand on others. The golden rule turned on its head could be: "I expect you to always love me as I love you," or even "I expect you to always love me as you love yourself."

These demands inevitably lead to disappointments, because we can only control our own behavior. Perhaps we can hope to set an attractive example that other people in our environment will want to emulate.

To mask our own ethical failures, we may even be heavy-handed with our demands. We may exhort others to be brave or merciful or loving or to practice other virtues. These exhortations may make us feel good, but without practicing the virtues in our own life, they do not help us to reach the Kingdom of God. When guiding others into virtues, we should show them the way, rather than preaching while setting a bad example. Jesus criticized scribes and Pharisees for this behavior:

> Then said Jesus to the crowds and to his disciples, "The scribes and the Pharisees sit on Moses' seat; so practice and observe whatever they tell you, but not what they do; for they preach, but do not practice. They bind heavy burdens, hard to bear, and lay them on men's shoulders; but they themselves will not move them with their finger." (Mt 23:1-4)

## 3.6 Stoicism and its Limits

In the ancient world, Stoicism was a school of thought that empha- sized virtues. The Stoic list of virtues significantly overlapped with the New Testament list because many virtues are universal and applicable in the pursuit of all big goals.

Today, some ethicists espouse a kind of neo-Stoicism, an ethics based on virtues. There is the stoic warrior (Sherman, 2005), Kipling's "Man" celebrated in the poem "If—," and Boy Scout Law. These and other systems often reflect the beauty of virtues and may present a good step toward embracing a full New Testament ethics.

However the question of virtues' purpose is the unsolved problem of Stoicism. If the purpose of a virtuous act is not a pleasure or the satisfaction, then what is it?

A statement, often attributed to Claudianus, gives the following answer: "Virtue is indeed its own reward." (*Ipsa qvidem pretivm virtvs sibi.*) In other words, virtue is an end in itself, a kind of behavioral adornment, something admirable like a beautiful ring on a finger. However when considering how difficult it is to live a life of virtue, this is not a satisfactory answer and a stronger motivation is necessary. The New Testament Ethics has an answer to this question in additional pillars that are missing in Stoicism. They are explained in the ensuing chapters.

## 3.7 Further Study

The list of virtues/prescriptions presented in this chapter is not meant to be complete. A great part of New Testament ethics deals with virtues/prescriptions and many additional virtues can be gleaned from it. Additional prescriptions are discussed in the rest of this book, including the Appendix.

St. Thomas Aquinas wrote in depth about virtues in *Summa Theologica*, Part 2.2. questions 1 – 170 (Aquinas, 1948). The Catechism of Catholic Church discusses the cardinal virtues of prudence/rationality, fortitude, justice, and temperance/moderation (CCC 1805–1809) and theological virtues of faith, hope, and love (CCC 1812-1832).

In many instances, the virtues that we called "reactive virtues" are called inaccurately "passive virtues." Pope Leo XIII criticized this notion (Leo, 1899), because there is nothing passive about them; they require substantial effort. Pope Leo XIII calls them "angelic" virtues, but that may sound quaint to our contemporary ears. This book calls them "reactive virtues," a more descriptive, but hopefully still accurate, term.

*Veritatis Splendor* contains extensive discussion of intrinsic evil (VS 56, 67, 80-83). Parents and educators who want to teach the life of virtue to their children can find a resource in specialized guides (Isaacs, 2001).

## Questions for Reflection or Group Discussion

1. Besides temperature control, list other practical situations where the reasoning about deficiency, excess, and optimum applies.

2. What is the role of feelings in moral decision-making?

3. What is the difference between proactive and reactive virtues?

4. Is it possible to reach the Kingdom of God without merciful justice?

5. What is the difference between humility and meekness?

6. How does the virtue of hope help us when doubts appear?

7. Give an example of intrinsic evil that is masked by a false virtue.

## References

Aquinas, T. (1948). *Summa Theologica*. New York: Benziger Bros.

Aristotle. Nicomachean ethics. In J. L. Ackrill (Ed.), *A New Aristotle Reader* (ppages 363 - 478). Princeton, N.J.: Princeton University Press.

Scout Law, https://www.scouting.org/discover/faq/question10/ (5/22/2018)

Isaacs, D. (2001). *Character Building: A Guide for Parents and Teachers*. Portland, OR: Four Courts Press.

Kipling, R. (1994). *The Collected Poems of Rudyard Kipling* Hertfordshire, UK: Wordsworth Editions.

Leo, X. (1899). Testem Benevolentiae. http://www.papalencyclicals.net/Leo13/l13teste.htm_(3/19/2016)

Robertson, D. (2013). *Stoicism and the Art of Happiness*. London: Hodder & Stoughton.

Sherman, N. (2005). *Stoic Warriors: The Ancient Philosophy behind the Military Mind*. Oxford University Press.

# 4
# *Priorities*

The previous chapters cover instructions how to avoid dangers and solve problems that we may encounter in the pursuit of big goals. However, we must also get our priorities straight. When Hannah drives to Chicago, she not only has to obey traffic rules and use skills that such a trip requires, but she also must not get distracted and abandon her goal. When Jacob works towards a bachelor's degree, he has to give priority to his studies and not allow distractions to displace them.

The same is true for the biggest goal, for our journey towards the Kingdom of God. The New Testament contains many pieces of advice how to prioritize so that we keep on the right path like Pavel Legerský did.

---

**▪ Different Words, Same Goal**

In the New Testament the Kingdom of God is called "Kingdom of heaven," "heaven," "eternal life," "great banquet," or "dwelling in Abraham's bosom." All these terms denote outcomes of a successful life. Reaching the Kingdom of God is called "salvation," as we already saw in the story of the rich young man. The invitation to the Kingdom of God is called "good news" or "glad tidings." The old English equivalent is *"god-spell"* and from that, we have the word "gospel." The Greek word *"evangelion"* is also commonly used.

Let us restate the reasons for pursuing the Kingdom of God. The Bible tells us that reaching the Kingdom of God exceeds all expectations (Lk 6:23, 1 Cor 2:9) while despair awaits people who fail (Lk 13:28). The divergent fates are contrasted in the parable of a rich man and Lazarus, in which a wealthy man heads for eternal condemnation, while a homeless and sick Lazarus reaches Abraham's bosom:

> *There was a rich man, who was clothed in purple and fine linen and who feasted sumptuously every day. And at his gate lay a poor man named Lazarus, full of sores, who desired to be fed with what fell from the rich man's table; moreover the dogs came and licked his sores. The poor man died and was carried by the angels to Abraham's bosom. The rich man also died and was buried; and in Hades, being in torment, he lifted up his eyes, and saw Abraham far off and Lazarus in his bosom. And he called out, 'Father Abraham, have mercy upon me, and send Lazarus to dip the end of his finger in water and cool my tongue; for I am in anguish in this flame.'*
>
> *But Abraham said, "Son, remember that you in your lifetime received your good things, and Lazarus in like manner evil things; but now he is comforted here, and you are in anguish. And besides all this, between us and you a great chasm has been fixed, in order that those who would pass from here to you may not be able, and none may cross from there to us." (Lk 16:19-26)*

There are many distractions on the path towards the Kingdom of God and *The First Commandment* is the concise expression of the priorities that we must maintain so we don't lose our way:

> *…Which commandment is the first of all? Jesus answered, the first is, 'Hear, O Israel: The Lord our God, the Lord is one; and you shall love the Lord your God with all your heart, and with all your soul, and with your entire mind, and with all your strength.' (Mk 12:28-30; see also Lk 10:27 and Mt 22:36-38)*

## 4.1 The Parable of the Sower

In the parable of sower, Jesus describes several ways how to think about the First Commandment:

> *A sower went out to sow his seed; and as he sowed, some fell along the path, and was trodden under foot, and the birds of the air devoured it. And some fell on the rock; and as it grew up, it withered away, because it had no moisture. And some fell among thorns; and the thorns grew with it and choked it. And some fell into good soil and grew, and yielded a hundredfold.... (Lk 8:5-8 see also Mt 13:3-9 and Mk 4:1-9)*

Later, Jesus elaborates on the meaning of this parable:

> *Now the parable is this: The seed is the word of God. The ones along the path are those who have heard; then the devil comes and takes away the word from their hearts, that they may not believe and be saved. And the ones on the rock are those who, when they hear the word, receive it with joy; but these have no root, they believe for a while and in time of temptation fall away. And as for what fell among the thorns, they are those who hear, but as they go on their way they are choked by the cares and riches and pleasures of life, and their fruit does not mature. And as for that in the good soil, they are those who, hearing the word, hold it fast in an honest and good heart, and bring forth fruit with patience. (Lk 8:11-15)*

So we see that those who receive the invitation to the Kingdom of God ("the seed") are divided into four broad groups:

- Those who reject the invitation immediately ("trodden under foot").
- Those who accept but lack perseverance when difficulties appear ("no root").
- Those who allow other lesser concerns to distract them ("the thorns choked it").

- The faithful disciples who maintain the right priorities and reach the Kingdom of God.

We will focus on each of these four groups separately in the rest of this chapter. Note that a variant of the parable of the sower applies to any big goal. If you do not accept the big goal ("trodden under foot"), or if you get scared away by difficulties ("no root"), or if you lose your priorities due to distractions ("the thorns choked it"), you will not reach your goal.

**Openness to the Invitation**

The first group ("seed trodden under foot") rejects the invitation immediately. This situation is noted in the New Testament in several places, where those invited treat the host with contempt and blatantly violate the First Commandment:

> *The kingdom of heaven may be compared to a king who gave a marriage feast for his son, and sent his servants to call those who were invited to the marriage feast; but they would not come. Again he sent other servants, saying, 'Tell those who are invited, behold, I have made ready my dinner, my oxen and my fat calves are killed, and everything is ready; come to the marriage feast.' But they made light of it and went off, one to his farm, another to his business, while the rest seized his servants, treated them shamefully, and killed them. (Mt 22:2-6, see also Mt 13:19-23, Mk 4:14-20)*

Searching for the Kingdom of God, like any big goal, requires free consent. It cannot be forced on anyone. The whole New Testament has a character of an invitation, an appeal to the free will of the reader or listener. As can be expected, there are people who reject that goal, who give greater priority to other things.

## Perseverance

The second group in the parable of sower consists of the people who approved of the First Commandment, enthusiastically accepting "the seed," but they do not persevere when serious difficulties come along. The New Testament characterizes them as having "no root" and lists tribulation and persecution as the leading reasons for their lack of perseverance. An analogy is a situation where Hannah, on the road to Chicago, stops at the Warren Dunes, finds the beach enticing, and gives up on the rest of the trip.

Our modern world is rarely receptive to the Gospels and puts negative pressure on us. This pressure ranges from a subtle form of disapproval to more serious forms, including societal persecution, as well as public censure. Some intolerant societies even go to the extreme of killing Christians and making them martyrs. The Gospels foresee this situation, likening Christians to sheep among wolves (Mt 10:16).

It is no surprise that in these circumstances, Christians often experience fear. That may be the primary reason why some people, in spite of their initial enthusiasm, turn away from pursuing their goal of reaching the Kingdom of God.

## 4.2 Distractions

The third group consists of the people who start well but at some point lose their way. The "thorns" of the parable of sower are the peripheral concerns that grow in their lives and overshadow Kingdom of God as their ultimate goal. An analogy is Hannah on the road to Chicago stops at the Warren Dunes, finds the beach enticing and gives up on the rest of the trip.

Many distractions on the path to the Kingdom of God have their origin in sins or lack of virtue that were already discussed in the previous chapters. However, serious distractions may also arise from good things that meet the criteria mentioned in the previous chapters, but have displaced God from the highest position and therefore contradict the First Commandment.

## Conflict of Priorities

In order to fulfill the First Commandment, we have to discern when the things of this world serve God and when they have become overgrown thorns in direct competition with God.

In popular language, the word "baggage" provides a useful analogy. When embarking on a long journey, we prudently bring along baggage that contains necessities for that trip. The longer the trip and the harsher the conditions we expect to find, the more baggage we carry.

However, our baggage may become an end in itself. Instead of concentrating on the goals of our trip, we focus on the baggage: How to acquire it, how to pack it, how to get it from one point to another or how to securely store it. In these circumstances, our baggage becomes our main concern, in effect completely displacing the reason for the trip. Thus, it's not surprising that "baggage" has acquired a second meaning in our modern culture, one synonymous with "liability." That is why we sometimes talk about politicians "carrying baggage" if they have acquired liabilities that may hurt their career.

When the baggage we need for our trip becomes an obstacle rather than a help, we face a crisis. Something useful has become a hindrance and so a new approach is required. The best way to handle baggage in such cases is to get rid of it, or at least reduce it by shipping it back, selling it, giving it away, or even throwing it away.

Books and movies present balloonists who carry various possessions in their gondola. But when their balloon begins leaking, they must throw some of their baggage overboard if they want to stay afloat. The same thing may happen with anything or anyone to whom we are attached; they can become "dead weight." It may happen with anything we possess or are related to. Anything of this world can become dead weight. If that happens, it has to be thrown overboard on our journey towards the Kingdom of God.

There are people who are unable to part with the cargo. In the end, though, they miss life's most important goal, as the earlier story of rich young man sadly illustrates (Mt 19:19-22). For this young man, his possessions may have served as very useful baggage in the past.

Perhaps his wealth protected him from many temptations and helped him to keep the prohibitions and prescriptions of the New Testament ethics. However, his possessions eventually became a liability when Jesus offered him the next step on his journey, and he had to decide whether to join Jesus and his closest disciples, or instead hang on to and manage his considerable material wealth. It was impossible to do both. Jesus asked him to take a step in faith similar to that which Peter, Andrew, James and John made in abandoning their fishing boats in order to join Jesus (Mt 4:18-22). Since the rich young man was unable to take that step, he missed a unique opportunity.

The First Commandment requires us to prudently recognize whether any earthly thing or relationship continues to lead us to the Kingdom of God or whether it has become an overgrown thorn. It also requires fortitude to change direction if necessary no matter how costly that can be. With some exaggeration, and therefore not to be taken literally, Jesus even talks about removing eyes and limbs if they become obstacles (Mk 9:43-47). The real point is that we have to be ready to part with any earthly good, or readjust or even end any relationship, if that is required by the First Commandment.

### ▪ Two Examples to Consider

Aron Ralston climbed alone in Bluejohn Canyon in Utah in April 2003. A large boulder shifted and pinned his right hand to the canyon wall. For several days, Aron tried to free himself without success. Facing certain death, he cut off much of his right forearm and by doing so saved his life (Benoist, 2010). This story was later turned into movie "127 hours." This is a dramatic example of a crucial decision made in a moment of crisis, as life has higher priority than a limb.

Now consider my father, who was born into a family of modest means. His studies at the Law School at Charles University in Prague required great sacrifices. Just before his graduation, he had to interrupt his studies for several years because Nazi occupiers closed all Czech universities. He finally received his degree after the defeat of Nazis in 1945, when Charles University reopened.

However, in 1948, there was a Communist coup and he faced a choice: Either to support the atheistic Communist regime and betray his love of God, or to be banned from the practice of law. In spite of all the sacrifices he made to earn his law degree, he chose what the love of God demanded and instead worked in blue collar professions. He valued his love of God more than his career in law. By doing so, he set an inspiring example on how to follow the First Commandment.

## Loving God above All Things

God must be our first priority. But that does not mean that earthly things and relationships should be neglected. We still must take care of them. As St. Paul counsels, "For everything created by God is good, and nothing is to be rejected if it is received with thanksgiving; for then it is consecrated by the word of God and prayer" (1 Tim 4:4-5).

In order to keep a proper perspective, we have to *strengthen our love of God*, so that the lure of earthly things and relationships does not overshadow our primary allegiance to God. St. Paul further advises, "So, whether you eat or drink, or whatever you do, do all to the glory of God" (1 Cor10:31).

As long as our activities ("whatever you do") do not involve sin, we can offer them for the glory of God. They then become a path to the Kingdom of God, rather than an obstacle, no matter how absorbing they are and how passionately we are involved in them. A short prayer before, during, or after any activity will be helpful to make that offering. This offering of one's effort to God and doing one's work well through the exercise of virtues is called *sanctification*. Even our other big goals can be sanctified and done for the glory of God. Hannah can sanctify her trip to Chicago and Jacob can sanctify his studies.

When interacting with people or things, we often become attached to them. This is natural, but we have to make sure that the strongest attachment in our lives remains our allegiance to God, as decreed by the First Commandment. *Detachment* is an effort to proactively weaken all earthly attachments so that they do not overshadow our love of God.

The New Testament contains a great example of detachment: St. John the Baptist. John led a life of austerity, living in the desert and eating only locusts and wild honey. This heroic detachment from creature comforts gave John the freedom to serve God wholeheartedly and to take uncompromising moral stands against worldly powers, even to the point of laying down his life (Mk 1:6, Lk 3:19, Mk 6:14-29, Lk 9:9). The New Testament makes clear that not everyone is called to a life of austerity like John's (Mt 11:18-19, Lk 7:33-34). However the prominent role St. John the Baptist plays in the New Testament reminds us that it is possible to detach from anything this world offers.

Jesus also exemplified detachment from earthly goods by fasting in preparation for his mission (Lk 4:1-2) and enduring deprivations in his single-minded focus on his ministry (Lk 9:58).

The New Testament provides a sober warning for us when dealing with some specific earthly goods. *Mammon* is the name given in the Gospels to money or other material possessions when we overvalue them and they hence become obstacles on our path towards the Kingdom of God: "No servant can serve two masters; for either he will hate the one and love the other, or he will be devoted to the one and despise the other. You cannot serve God and mammon" (Lk 16:13). Money is an earthly good with a very strong "pull" and St. Paul teaches, "the love of money is the root of all evils" (1 Tim 16:10).

In trying to determine whether our financial resources or other material goods are necessary to accomplish worthwhile goals, or whether we deal with mammon, the New Testament offers this guidepost: "For where your treasure is, there will your heart be also" (Mt 6:21). The "heart" in this context means our dreams and desires, which reveal whether we are oriented primarily towards God or something or someone else. Our dreams and desires reveal what motivates us most, what guides our decisions, and therefore what is our likely destiny. Excessive concern about any earthly treasure is unhealthy and has to be subjugated to the First Commandment. That is the only way how to journey towards the Kingdom of God.

*Power and fame* are other examples of earthly goods that have a strong allure. St. Mother Teresa and Pope St. John Paul II showed that these gifts can be sanctified. They both attained the status of media stars and used that position to spread the Gospel by both their teachings and by the example of their lives. However, people who pursue power or glory for their own sake, rather than as a tool to bring others to God, live a seriously disordered life: "How can you believe, who receive glory from one another and do not seek the glory that comes from the only God?" (Jn 5:44).

Detachment from money and other earthly concerns can be a great help in living the First Commandment, but must be exercised with caution. It always has to involve God as a superior life-guiding choice, otherwise, it can become just an excuse for laziness.

## 4.3 "Good Soil"

The final group noted in the parable of the sower is characterized as seed that falls on "good soil." The people who belong to this group accept the seed (God's word), allow it to grow, and return a great harvest, a hundredfold yield. The Gospels refers to people in this final group as "blessed" (Mt 5:1-12).

### Beatitudes

The traveler nearing the Kingdom of God needs signposts that indicate how far away their goal is; these signposts are collectively called "the Beatitudes." The Beatitudes highlight specific accomplishments in living New Testament Ethics, reflecting how far we have come and how far we still have to go in attaining the Kingdom of God (Mt 5:1-12):

- *"Blessed are the poor in spirit, for theirs is the kingdom of heaven"* (Mt 5:3). This beatitude praises those who are detached from material things ("poor in spirit"), do not long for anything material and are ready to part with any material possessions if necessary. They are free from the domination of the things of this earth; Jesus sets that example par excellence (Lk 9:58).

- *"Blessed are those who mourn, for they shall be comforted"* (Mt 5:4). This beatitude results from an internalized love of our neighbor. There is a lot of misery in the world and a lot of ill-conceived plans that, if not stopped, are certain to end in grief. The blessed ones know that and mourn. Jesus gives an example of this beatitude: ". . . he drew near and saw the city he wept over it, saying, 'Would that even today you knew the things that make for peace! But now they are hid from your eyes. . .'" (Luke 19:41-42). Note that mourning also can be a result of narcissistic self-pity, but this beatitude is a far cry from that; this is a celebration of empathy. During his passion, Jesus never cried over his own suffering but rather interceded for his persecutors, setting an example for all in living this beatitude (Lk 24:34).

- *"Blessed are the meek, for they shall inherit the earth"* (Mt 5:5). This is the beatitude of people who have internalized the virtue of meekness, who are patient with others and avoid unnecessary strife. Jesus exemplifies this beatitude when not arguing with the chief priests in the presence of Herod, even at the cost of his reputation: "When Herod saw Jesus, he was very glad, for he had long desired to see him, because he had heard about him, and he was hoping to see some sign done by him. So he questioned him at some length; but he made no answer. The chief priests and the scribes stood by, vehemently accusing him. And Herod with his soldiers treated him with contempt and mocked him . . ." (Lk 23:8-11).

- *"Blessed are those who hunger and thirst for righteousness, for they shall be satisfied"* (Mt 5:6). Translated into the contemporary language, these blessed ones strive ("hunger and thirst") to live a morally upright life, one that is in full accord

61

with the New Testament demands. Jesus was known to be righteous, as testified by Pilate's wife: "Have nothing to do with that righteous man. I suffered much in a dream today because of him" (Mt 27:29).

- *"Blessed are the merciful, for they shall obtain mercy"* (Mt 5:7). These blessed ones personify the virtue of mercy; they no longer have to struggle with each act of mercy, because mercy has become a habit for them. Jesus exercised mercy many times in his life; for example, when he healed the sick or when he prayed for the Roman soldiers who carried out his crucifixion: "Father, forgive them; for they know not what they do" (Lk 23:34).

- *"Blessed are the pure in heart, for they shall see God"* (Mt 5:8). Here, "pure" means "clean" or "clear." The blessed ones act with great integrity and serve the Lord unselfishly. They also excel in chastity, not only in their outward actions but also in their innermost thoughts.

- *"Blessed are the peacemakers, for they shall be called sons of God"* (Mt 5:9). The peacemakers possess God's gift of inner peace which motivates all of their actions in fostering the peace in the world. This profound inner peace guides them through all their sufferings and misfortunes, no matter how dire. They know that everything will ultimately be all right: "I have said these things to you, that in me you may have peace. In the world you will have tribulation. But take heart; I have overcome the world" (Jn 16:33).

- *"Blessed are those who are persecuted for righteousness' sake, for theirs is the kingdom of heaven. Blessed are you when men revile you and persecute you and utter all kinds of evil against you falsely on my account. Rejoice and be glad, for your reward is great in heaven, for so men persecuted the prophets who were before you"* (Mt 5:10-12).

This is the beatitude of the courageous ones. They do not hesitate to publicly respond to the call for justice and often encounter the wrath of the powerful and of society in general. This beatitude is an honest assessment of what living the New Testament Ethics also means. From a purely earthly perspective, it often results in trouble. This fact is acknowledged in popular wisdom by the cynical comment, "No good deed goes unpunished." Jesus puts it in this way: "If the world hates you, realize that it hated me first. If you belonged to the world, the world would love its own; but because you do not belong to the world, and I have chosen you out of the world, the world hates you" (Jn 15:18-19).

The Beatitudes are signposts. If you are nearing the Kingdom of God, living in conformity with New Testament ethics, you can check which beatitudes you are living well and those where do you still have room for progress.

Note that for any big goal, there will be signs when the seeker successfully approaches it. Consider these examples:

Jacob is close to successfully completing his bachelor's degree in computer science if:

- Instead of accepting an invitation to a party, he enjoys debugging his programming assignment that is due next week.
- Sometimes Jacob overhears other people referring to him as "that nerd."
- Jacob's circle of friends expands as they seek his help prior to the due date for the next assignment.

Hannah may be getting close to her destination in Chicago if:

- She is stuck in a traffic jam.
- The drivers around her are behaving unpredictably and she must pay closer attention not only to the car in front of her, but also the cars on both sides of her, as well as cars behind.
- She can see the skyscrapers of the Chicago Loop ahead and the blue waters of Lake Michigan on her right.

## Merit

From time immemorial, people were puzzled by the mystery of death and asked what they could take with them into eternal life. A popular mistake is to assert that we cannot take anything with us and so we better enjoy life while we're still alive.

The New Testament counters that there are things that count even after death, but we have to be very careful what we invest into while here on earth: "Do not lay up for yourselves treasures on earth, where moth and rust consume and where thieves break in and steal, but lay up for yourselves treasures in heaven, where neither moth nor rust consumes and where thieves do not break in and steal" (Mt 6:19-20).

The things that can become "treasures in heaven" are collectively called "merits," similar to merit badges earned in Boy Scouts. However, spiritual merits are of much greater and lasting value. The Gospels list several ways how to gain merits.

The last beatitude states that persecution for Gospel's sake is one of the merits that can be taken from this world to the next, "for your reward is great in heaven" (Mt 5:12). Acts of mercy also gain merit: "For truly, I say to you, whoever gives you a cup of water to drink because you belong to Christ will by no means lose his reward" (Mt 10:42). Almsgiving is another meritorious act: "Sell your possessions, and give alms; provide yourselves with purses that do not grow old, with a treasure in the heavens that does not fail, where no thief approaches and no moth destroys. For where your treasure is, there will your heart be also" (Lk 12:33-34).

Also every sacrifice made in following Jesus will be "repaid" as merits: "And everyone who has left houses or brothers or sisters or father or mother or children or lands, for my name's sake, will receive a hundredfold, and inherit eternal life" (Mt 19:29; see also Lk 18:29-30).

However, we must do good deeds for the right reason; otherwise, they will not gain merit. They must be done out of love of God and neighbor, and certainly not for show, as the Gospels make very clear:

*Beware of practicing your piety before men in order to be seen by them; for then you will have no reward from your Father who is in heaven. Thus, when you give alms, sound no trumpet before you, as the hypocrites do in the synagogues and in the streets, that they may be praised by men. Truly, I say to you, they have received their reward. But when you give alms, do not let your left hand know what your right hand is doing, so that your alms may be in secret; and your Father who sees in secret will reward you. (Mt 6:1-4)*

We must perform our good deeds with a spirit of humility, otherwise, they are not meritorious. We must always remember that it is God who grants merits. We do not earn them on our own:

*Two men went up into the temple to pray, one a Pharisee and the other a tax collector. The Pharisee stood and prayed thus with himself, 'God, I thank thee that I am not like other men, extortioners, unjust, adulterers, or even like this tax collector. I fast twice a week, I give tithes of all that I get.' But the tax collector, standing far off, would not even lift up his eyes to heaven, but beat his breast, saying, 'God, be merciful to me a sinner!' I tell you, this man went down to his house justified rather than the other; for every one who exalts himself will be humbled, but he who humbles himself will be exalted. (Lk 18:10-14)*

## 4.4  More on Reasoning about Priorities

In the context of the First Commandment, we reason about our acts by answering the following questions: "Is this act displacing my love of God? Have I lowered my sights and instead of worshiping God, do I worship something of this earth?" Specific examples are: "Am I attached to money, to fame, to health, to success, to family, to a neighbor . . . (fill in any other good thing or person), to the point that it overshadows my love of God? Am I so strongly attached to something or someone in this world that, in a crisis situation, I would likely choose it over God?" If the answer to any of these questions is "Yes," then we are have a problem and we need to correct our attitude.

Reasoning about the First Commandment is very different than the reasoning about the rules of the previous two pillars. In this case, there is no precipice to stay far away from, and there is no optimum to search for and no excess to avoid. In loving God, more is always better.

In summary, New Testament Ethics demands that God always be first in our lives. However, note that love of God manifests itself in love of our neighbor, as discussed in this and the previous chapters.

## 4.5 Pelagianism and its Limits

In this and previous chapters, we have emphasized the human effort that living the New Testament Ethics requires. Although human capabilities are great, there are always limits. That raises these questions: Are the goals of the New Testament Ethics beyond these limits?

Some of the New Testament rules are very demanding and hard to fulfill. What happens when they are not fulfilled? What if somebody cannot go any further and is still far away from the Kingdom of God? What happens when somebody stumbles and falls, is all lost? Do we have assistance to get up and to overcome defects, or are we on our own?

The incomplete ethics that relies on human effort only has been called "Pelagianism," named after the English monk Pelagius who taught in Rome in the late 4th and early 5th centuries. Pelagius erroneously taught that natural human capabilities are sufficient to reach the Kingdom of God and missed the help that we need from God. That help from God is the remaining pillar of the New Testament Ethics. It is covered in the next chapter.

## 4.6 Further Study

In *Jesus of Nazareth*, Pope Benedict XVI (2007) discusses the Beatitudes at great length. Pope St. John Paul II emphasizes "following

Jesus" as the key to keeping the demands of the New Testament Ethics (VS 19-21). In *Friends of God,* St. Josemaria Escriva explores the importance of the First Commandment in relationship to our earthly role and teaches lay spirituality that allows busy people to be both fully immersed in the world and at the same time keep the First Commandment (Escriva, 1981).

The Catechism of the Catholic Church discusses merits (CCC 2006-2011). The story of Pelagius and his errors is explained in *Pelagius and Pelagianism* (Pohle, 1911).

The Pelagian view assumes that Christians can reach their own earthly goals—and even heaven—by using simply their own effort and natural capabilities. This view reappears in much of modern "goal setting" literature that explores the human capacities. However it often shows a blind spot for the importance of God's role in our life (Locke & Latham, 2002). Much of today's self-improvement literature suffers from the same omission.

## Questions for Reflection or Group Discussion

1.  What are the contrasting outcomes of human life?

2.  Why is it impossible to have several most important goals in your life? What is your most important goal?

3.  What are the main obstacles on the path to reaching the Kingdom of God? What obstacles are in *your own* path?

4.  Name some earthly goods that are synergistic with our primary duty to keep the First Commandment. How do you sanctify them? At what point might they become obstacles?

5.  Have you or people you know experienced a call to do more for God? How have you (they) responded? Have you (they) missed an opportunity?

6.  Can you distinguish serving God authentically vs. a show of vanity (pride)? What are the telling/distinguishing signs?

## References

Benedict, XVI. (2007). *Jesus of Nazareth: From the Baptism in the Jordan to the Transfiguration.* Trans. Adrian J. Walker. New York: Doubleday.

Benoist, M. (2010). *Climber Who Cut Off Hand Looks Back.* National Geographic News. http://news.nationalgeographic.com/news/2004/08/0830_040830_aronralston.html (8/29/2014)

Escriva, J. (2017). *Christ is Passing By*: Scepter Publishers.

Locke, E. A., & Latham, G. P. (2002). *Building a Practically Useful Theory of Goal Setting and Task Motivation: A 35-Year Odyssey.* American Psychologist, 57(9), 705.

Pohle, J. (1911). *Pelagius and Pelagianism.* The Catholic Encyclopedia. http://www.newadvent.org/cathen/11604a.htm (3/8/2012)

# 5
# *Providence and Grace*

Success of our earthly goals depends not only on our own effort, but also on external factors. For example, Hannah's trip to Chicago can be successful only if the roads are in good shape, a conscientious mechanic maintains her car, and well-supplied gas stations operate along the roads.

External help is essential on our journey towards the Kingdom of God. Remember that when the apostles hear the explanation of what that journey requires, they wonder whether it is possible at all. Jesus reassures them: "With men this is impossible, but with God all things are possible" (Mt 19:25-26). God's gifts give us a hope that we can reach the Kingdom of God. These gifts are the fourth pillar of New Testament Ethics.

## 5.1 God's Gifts: Natural and Supernatural

God makes all things possible through His gifts. Some gifts are *natural*; among them, reason and free will play the central role in ethics and have already been discussed in the previous chapters. Some people have received additional natural gifts: They may be physically strong, or are artistic, or have analytical abilities, and so forth. Other natural gifts are the external support they receive from the world around them, whether it's their family, acquaintances, neighbors, co-workers, institutions, economy, government, and the world's resources. These natural gifts are parts of *God's providence*.

Many people have achieved remarkable feats in science, engineering, arts, economics, politics or other areas by cultivating and exercising their natural gifts. For earthly goals like the trip to Chicago or studying for a bachelor's degree, natural gifts are necessary and they are available to many. However, there are limits to what we can accomplish with our natural endowments. Reaching the Kingdom of God is beyond our natural capabilities and we need extra help from God.

> ### ▪ Futile Earthly Quests
>
> The rich and powerful sometimes fail to see their natural limits. They often wrongly think that they can take care of everything through their own efforts and possessions. The desire for immortality is strong, and there are wealthy and powerful people who have tried to overcome death through natural means that range from ridiculous to bizarre.
>
> Qin Shi Huang was the first emperor of China. He conquered "warring kingdoms" and created a huge Chinese empire. He unified it both administratively and culturally and constructed the Great Wall to protect it. The only thing that Qin Shi Huang feared was his own death. In anticipation, he built a huge tomb guarded by more than 8,000 life-size terracotta soldiers. It is one of the wonders of the world and a testimony to how far Qin Shi Huang was willing to go in order to immortalize himself.
>
> The Pharaohs of Egypt built pyramids in order to keep their name forever alive. Medieval rich men were seeking the "fountain of youth" that would keep them forever young. In more recent times, science is expected to deliver eternal life (SENS Research Foundation). In the meantime, while science is still working on it, wealthy people can store their frozen cadaver and wait for scientific progress to take place. They hope that if science solves the problem of immortality, their frozen bodies will be unfrozen and they will be brought to life and live forever (Cryonics Institute).

*Grace* is the additional and supernatural gift of God that perfects our natural gifts and helps where they fail. We need it to reach the Kingdom of God. We can receive it through Jesus and his Church. Hence Jesus is not only our teacher, but also the source of grace: "For the law was given through Moses; grace and truth came through Jesus Christ" (Jn 1:17). We know that natural gifts are given to people in different measures. Likewise, God's graces are also distributed unevenly. And yet, God in his infinite love desires that *all human beings be saved* (1 Tim 2:4, 2 Pet 3:9).

> ▪ **Long Studies of Providence and Grace**
>
> God's providence and grace are central topics of theology. There is a considerable amount of theological literature that deals with them, including the early Church Fathers and medieval scholars. In disputes between Protestants and Catholics, the understanding of providence and grace became one of the central issues. Today's theology provides additional insights. For our discussion of the introductory New Testament Ethics, the notions of providence and grace are sufficient. "God's blessing" or "God's gift" is sometimes used as synonyms for both providence and grace.

God is generous with His blessings. As St. Paul writes: "And God is able to provide you with every blessing in abundance, so that you may always have enough of everything and may provide in abundance for every good work" (2 Cor 9:8).

## Infused virtues

While some of the virtues that were covered in previous chapters are based on our natural gifts (called "human virtues"), others require grace. They are called "infused virtues" and all theological virtues are infused.

*Faith* is an infused virtue because it is a gift from God, explained in the following way: "You did not choose me, but I chose you..."

(Jn 15:16). "Conversion" is a reception of that gift. St. Paul is a prime example of conversion:

*Now as he journeyed he approached Damascus, and suddenly a light from heaven flashed about him. And he fell to the ground and heard a voice saying to him, "Saul, Saul, why do you persecute me?" And he said, "Who are you, Lord?" And he said, "I am Jesus, whom you are persecuting; but rise and enter the city, and you will be told what you are to do." The men who were traveling with him stood speechless, hearing the voice but seeing no one. Saul arose from the ground; and when his eyes were opened, he could see nothing; so they led him by the hand and brought him into Damascus. And for three days he was without sight, and neither ate nor drank.*

*Now there was a disciple at Damascus named Ananias. The Lord said to him in a vision, "Ananias." And he said, "Here I am, Lord." And the Lord said to him, "Rise and go to the street called Straight, and inquire in the house of Judas for a man of Tarsus named Saul; for behold, he is praying, and he has seen a man named Ananias come in and lay his hands on him so that he might regain his sight." But Ananias answered, "Lord, I have heard from many about this man, how much evil he has done to thy saints at Jerusalem; and here he has authority from the chief priests to bind all who call upon thy name." But the Lord said to him, "Go, for he is a chosen instrument of mine to carry my name before the Gentiles and kings and the sons of Israel; for I will show him how much he must suffer for the sake of my name."*

*So Ananias departed and entered the house. And laying his hands on him he said, "Brother Saul, the Lord Jesus who appeared to you on the road by which you came, has sent me that you may regain your sight and be filled with the Holy Spirit." And immediately something like scales fell from his eyes and he regained his sight. Then he rose and was baptized, and took food and was strengthened. For several days he was with the disciples at Damascus. And in the synagogues immediately he proclaimed*

*Jesus, saying, "He is the Son of God." And all who heard him were amazed, and said, "Is not this the man who made havoc in Jerusalem of those who called on this name? And he has come here for this purpose, to bring them bound before the chief priests." But Saul increased all the more in strength, and confounded the Jews who lived in Damascus by proving that Jesus was the Christ. (Acts 9:3-22)*

Conversion can be as dramatic as St. Paul experienced, or more subtle. All believers have a moment or sequence of moments when the "scales fell from their eyes" and they started believing. Often they remember that moment as one of the most important moments of their life.

*Hope* is also an infused virtue. There is a natural reason to cling to hope: Hope brings peace into our life; without it, life would be miserable and big goals would be unreachable. However, mere natural hope is insufficient during times of great trials and in trying to reach the Kingdom of God (Rom 15:13).

*Love* is another infused virtue. Our nature is usually sufficient for loving friends and relatives; this is even reflected in language where relatives are often called "loved ones." However the New Testament counsels to "love one's enemies." That is a much more difficult task. It looks illogical, perhaps dangerous, to love enemies because doing so may leave us vulnerable. Therefore, we need a love that exceeds our natural strength: "For if you love those who love you, what reward have you?" Jesus asks. "Do not even the tax collectors do the same?" (Mt 5:46).

## Consolations

When pursuing big goals, there are encouragements along the way. For example, stopping at Warren Dunes at Lake Michigan is a break for Hannah on the long trip to Chicago. The joy of the first working software project encourages Jacob in the studies towards a bachelor's degree in computer science. The memory of one's honeymoon is an encouragement on the long journey of marriage. And the first smile of a child is an encouragement along the challenging path of parenthood.

Consolations are encouragements from God, sent to weary pilgrims along their arduous path. Inner peace is one such consolation that is often mentioned in the New Testament (Jn 14:27, 16:33) and that Pavel Legerský so clearly demonstrated. The second beatitude mentions comfort as another consolation that the pilgrims experience (Mt 5:4). So does St. Paul:

*Blessed be the God and Father of our Lord Jesus Christ, the Father of mercies and God of all comfort, who comforts us in all our affliction, so that we may be able to comfort those who are in any affliction, with the comfort with which we ourselves are comforted by God. For as we share abundantly in Christ's sufferings, so through Christ we share abundantly in comfort too. If we are afflicted, it is for your comfort and salvation; and if we are comforted, it is for your comfort, which you experience when you patiently endure the same sufferings that we suffer. Our hope for you is unshaken; for we know that as you share in our sufferings, you will also share in our comfort. (2 Cor 1:3–7)*

> ▪ **Bearing the Ridicule**
>
> The eternal life promised by the New Testament is often—unsurprisingly—ridiculed by people without faith. After all, God and heaven are invisible and beyond our earthly experience. However, even the earthly gift of comfort and inner peace of the faithful is mocked by some. Karl Marx called religion (read Christianity) the "opium of the people." By that, he implied the inner peace that Christianity offers is useless and even harmful. Instead, he offered activism driven by class hatred. The Communist regimes that sprang from his thought committed atrocities crying to heaven, the bitter fruit of that recommendation.

## God's Forgiveness

Seeking the Kingdom of God is a demanding project. Although there is the help of God's grace, there are inevitable stumbles that result in sins. Sin, even mortal sin, does not have to spell the end of our attempt to reach the Kingdom of God. God's forgiveness provides a new start that allows us to reach our goal, the Kingdom of God.

> ▪ **Stumbling and Forgiveness**
>
> Demanding goals can be reached only when the stumbles of the past are forgiven. For example, expiration of a driver's previous penalty points that were accumulated by traffic rules violations, allows many people to drive. Without such forgiveness, many would not be able to drive because of a license suspension. For undergraduate students, extra credits or a possibility to repeat failed classes allows them to make up for their academic failures and earn their degrees.

The New Testament explains that the power to forgive sins is fully vested in Jesus of Nazareth:

> *On one of those days, as he was teaching, there were Pharisees and teachers of the law sitting by, who had come from every village of Galilee and Judea and from Jerusalem; and the power of the Lord was with him to heal. And behold, men were bringing on a bed a man who was paralyzed, and they sought to bring him in and lay him before Jesus; but finding no way to bring him in, because of the crowd, they went up on the roof and let him down with his bed through the tiles into the midst before Jesus.*
> *And when he saw their faith he said, "Man, your sins are forgiven you." And the scribes and the Pharisees began to question, saying, "Who is this that speaks blasphemies? Who can forgive sins but God only?" When Jesus perceived their questionings, he answered them, "Why do you question in your hearts? Which is easier, to say, 'Your sins are forgiven you,' or to say, 'Rise and walk? But that you may know that the Son of man has authority*

*on earth to forgive sins"—he said to the man who was para-lyzed—"I say to you, rise, take up your bed and go home." And immediately he rose before them, and took up that on which he lay, and went home, glorifying God. (Lk 5:17-25)*

Jesus delegated this awesome power to the apostles and the Church:

*And when he had said this, he breathed on them, and said to them, "Receive the Holy Spirit. If you forgive the sins of any, they are forgiven; if you retain the sins of any, they are retained." (Jn 20:22-23)*

However, we must repent to have our sins forgiven:

*"I tell you, No; but unless you repent you will all likewise perish. Or those eighteen upon whom the tower in Siloam fell and killed them, do you think that they were worse offenders than all the others who dwelt in Jerusalem? I tell you, No; but unless you repent you will all likewise perish." (Lk 13:3-5)*

People who have committed venial sins, or mortal sins for which they have repented, can still reach heaven, although through the intermediate, after-death purification called *Purgatory*. The New Testament explains purgatory through the analogy of fire, which tests all deeds. The good deeds are likened to fire resistant material, while imperfect deeds are likened to flammable material and turn into a loss. However the sinner still is saved, although through the pain of fire:

*Now if any one builds on the foundation with gold, silver, precious stones, wood, hay, straw—each man's work will become manifest; for the Day will disclose it, because it will be revealed with fire, and the fire will test what sort of work each one has done. If the work which any man has built on the foundation survives, he will receive a reward. If any man's work is burned up, he will suffer loss, though he himself will be saved, but only as through fire. (1 Cor 3:12-15)*

## 5.2 Responding to God's Grace

Since God's gifts are received and not earned, reactive virtues play the fundamental role in their reception. Humility is necessary in order to receive and value them (Heb. 4:6). Gratitude is necessary to acknowledge the giver. Flexibility is necessary to make full use of the unexpected gifts. Well-behaved little children know how to receive gifts with natural humility and serve as an example (Mt 18:1-4).

We should take good care of God's gifts; there is always a danger that these gifts may be lost through foolishness or neglect. Note there is an asymmetry in God's gifts: We do not have the power to earn them, but we have the damaging power to lose them through wrong acts or passivity.

### Seeking Grace

The New Testament provides many instances in which people seek God's gifts, including natural blessings like health. The New Testament praises them and presents them as examples to emulate (Mt 9:20, Mk 5:21-34, Luke 8:43-48).

Grace is an essential ingredient in our pursuit of eternal life. However, since we cannot earn grace, the question arises: Is there anything that we can do, besides passively waiting? The answer is that while it is not possible to earn the grace, it is still possible to ask God for grace. Jesus is very encouraging in this respect:

> *Ask, and it will be given you; seek, and you will find; knock, and it will be opened to you. For every one who asks receives, and he who seeks finds, and to him who knocks it will be opened. Or what man of you, if his son asks him for bread, will give him a stone? Or if he asks for a fish, will give him a serpent? If you then, who are evil, know how to give good gifts to your children, how much more will your Father who is in heaven give good things to those who ask him! (Mt 7:7-11)*

*Prayer* is a fundamental and particularly effective way to seek grace. Prayer is our conversation with God, and Jesus provides great examples of frequent prayer. He prayed before every important decision, for example, before choosing his apostles (Lk 6:12-19). He prayed in difficult situations, when his enemies were plotting against him (Lk 22:41-44). And he also prayed when he humanly needed a break (Mk 1:35, Mt 14:23).

*Vocal prayer* is a prayer expressed in words. The Lord's Prayer is a vocal prayer that Jesus gave us:

> *"Our Father who art in heaven, Hallowed be thy name. Thy kingdom come. Thy will be done, On earth as it is in heaven. Give us this day our daily bread; And forgive us our debts, As we also have forgiven our debtors; And lead us not into temptation, But deliver us from evil." (Mt 6:9-13)*

*Meditation* is a prayer where we use our own words, thoughts, imagination or other mental faculties and share with God matters we consider important. An example is in Jesus' prayer in the Garden of Gethsemane (Mt 26:36-46).

Note again that faith is a crucial virtue, because it opens the door to the reception of graces: "For God so loved the world, as to give his only-begotten Son; that whosoever believeth in him, may not perish, but may have life everlasting" (Jn 3:16). In prayer, we can ask for an increase in faith. We are encouraged by the example of a father of an afflicted son who cried out to Jesus, "I believe, help my unbelief" (Mk 9:24).

*The sacraments of the Church* are the primary source of grace. Jesus exhorts the apostles and the Church: "Go therefore and make disciples of all nations, baptizing them in the name of the Father and of the Son and of the Holy Spirit" (Mt 28:19) and ". . . repentance and forgiveness of sins should be preached in his name to all nations" (Lk 24:47).

## Promptings of Grace

Seeking grace is our task, but it is comforting to know that Jesus also seeks us. This increases the possibility that we will connect: "Behold, I stand at the door and knock; if any one hears my voice and opens the door, I will come in to him and eat with him, and he with me" (Rev 3:20). The parable of the lost sheep provides further encouragement (Lk 15:1-7).

This "knocking on the door" is called an *inspiration* or *prompting of grace*. It can be a good idea that appears in our mind and if followed, leads to a good outcome. Or, an inspiring event opens up unexpected possibilities. The New Testament describes miraculous cures that not only alleviated suffering, but also inspired the witnesses into believing the power of God (Heb 2:4).

## Persistence

The New Testament contains numerous passages where the reader is exhorted to be persistent in search of grace and not to become discouraged. It is illustrated in the parable of the persistent widow:

> And he told them a parable, to the effect that they ought always to pray and not lose heart. He said, "In a certain city there was a judge who neither feared God nor regarded man; and there was a widow in that city who kept coming to him and saying, 'Vindicate me against my adversary.' For a while he refused; but afterward he said to himself, 'Though I neither fear God nor regard man, yet because this widow bothers me, I will vindicate her, or she will wear me out by her continual coming.'" And the Lord said, "Hear what the unrighteous judge says. And will not God vindicate his elect, who cry to him day and night? Will he delay long over them? I tell you, he will vindicate them speedily." (Lk 18: 1-8)

God's mercy is so generous that it is *never too late* to repent. There are workers in the vineyard who—although late—are paid the full wage for their effort (Mt 20:1-8). The New Testament presents the good thief, who converts from a life of sin literally minutes before his death, and yet he is promised life in heaven:

*Now one of the criminals hanging there reviled Jesus, saying, "Are you not the Messiah? Save yourself and us." The other, however, rebuking him, said in reply, "Have you no fear of God, for you are subject to the same condemnation? And indeed, we have been condemned justly, for the sentence we received corresponds to our crimes, but this man has done nothing criminal." Then he said, "Jesus, remember me when you come into your kingdom." He replied to him, "Amen I say to you today you will be with me in Paradise." (Lk 23:39-43)*

This biblical story needs to be read with caution. There is never a guarantee that there will be such a great gift of grace at the very last moment of our life. In psychological terms, the good thief had to reject a substantial part his life that was based on crime, and he had to overcome all his rationalizations and attachments, before he was ready to make his bold request.

This biblical story is not there to encourage us to postpone conversion, but it serves as an encouragement that the goal of eternal life is never completely lost, no matter how bleak the situation may seem. By contrast, the parable of the wise and foolish virgins illustrates people who missed their chance and when they wake up to the reality, it is too late:

*Then the kingdom of heaven shall be compared to ten maidens who took their lamps and went to meet the bridegroom. Five of them were foolish, and five were wise. For when the foolish took their lamps, they took no oil with them; but the wise took flasks of oil with their lamps. As the bridegroom was delayed, they all slumbered and slept. But at midnight there was a cry, 'Behold, the bridegroom! Come out to meet him.' Then all those maidens rose and trimmed their lamps. And the foolish said to the wise, 'Give us some of your oil, for our lamps are going out.' But the wise replied, 'Perhaps there will not be enough for us and for you; go rather to the dealers and buy for yourselves.' And while they went to buy, the bridegroom came, and those who were ready went in with him to the marriage feast; and the door was shut. Afterward the other maidens came also, saying, 'Lord, lord, open to us.' But he replied, 'Truly, I say to you, I do not know you.' Watch therefore, for you know neither the day nor the hour. (Mt 25: 1-13)*

It is never too late to seek grace. There are examples where grace has been received by people very late in life. On the other hand, it is prudent to eagerly accept God's grace whenever He provides it to us, whether early or late, and then hold on it because there may be no second chance.

## 5.3  More on Reasoning about Providence and Grace

St. Augustine is called "the Doctor of Grace" because he extensively studied the subject of God's grace. He expressed the balance between our natural gifts and God's grace this way: "God therefore does not command impossibilities; but in His command He counsels you both to do what you can for yourself, and to ask His aid in what you cannot do." If we cannot perform acts that are mandated on our path towards the Kingdom of God, or abstain from prohibited acts, we have to rely on God's grace and seek it with humility and persistence.

> ### ▪ Twelve-step Programs
>
> Twelve-step programs, originally made famous by Alcoholics Anonymous, address acts which are necessary, but we seem to be unable to do them on our own. There may be temptations that are stronger than our will and alcoholics or other addicts experience such temptations. The 12 steps are:
>
> - Step 1 – Powerlessness. We admitted we were powerless over our addiction—that our lives had become unmanageable.
> - Step 2 – Hope. We came to believe that a Power greater than ourselves could restore us to sanity.

- Step 3 – Decision. We made a decision to turn our will and our lives over to the care of God as we understood God

- Step 4 – Inventory. We made a searching and fearless moral inventory of ourselves

- Step 5 – Confession. We admitted to God, to ourselves and to another human being the exact nature of our wrongs

- Step 6 – Readiness. We were entirely ready to have God remove all these defects of character

- Step 7 – Asked God. We humbly asked God to remove our shortcomings

- Step 8 – Amends List. We made a list of all persons we had harmed, and became willing to make amends to them all

- Step 9 – Amends. We made direct amends to such people wherever possible, except when to do so would injure them or others

- Step 10 – Inventory. We continued to take personal inventory and when we were wrong promptly admitted it

- Step 11 – Keep Contact. We sought through prayer and meditation to improve our conscious contact with God as we understood God, praying only for knowledge of God's will for us and the power to carry that out

- Step 12 – Help Others. Having had a spiritual awakening as the result of these steps, we tried to carry this message to other addicts, and to practice these principles in all our affairs.

Reprinted from "The 12 Steps."

## 5.4 Further Study

God's grace and providence is a vast theological topic. Besides the seminal work of St. Augustine, there are many theological publications that discuss God's providence and grace. The Church confirmed the insight of St. Augustine at the Council of Trent (Paul III). The *Catechism of Catholic Church* addresses extensively the subjects of providence (CCC 301 – 314), grace (CCC 1996-2005), prayer (CCC 2558-2865) and sacraments (CCC 1210-1666). Pope St. John Paul II points out that grace is necessary for everyone who wants to follow the New Testament Ethics (VS 24, 104-105).

## Questions for Reflection or Group Discussion

1. What is the difference between natural gifts and grace? Why do we need both?

2. How do we obtain grace? Can we earn it?

3. Which virtues are infused?

4. What virtues are necessary to receive God's grace?

5. How do we deal with tasks that are necessary on our path towards Kingdom of God, but at the same time are so difficult that they seem to be impossible?

## References

*The 12 Steps* http://12step.org/the-12-steps/ (4/12/2016).

Augustine. *Of Nature and Grace* http://www.logoslibrary.org/augustine/nature/43.html (4/12/2016).

Cryonics institute http://www.cryonics.org/ (4/12/2016).

Paul III. *Decree Concerning Justification, Chapter IX.* http://www.ewtn.com/library/councils/trent6.htm (4/12/2016).

SENS research foundation http://www.sens.org/ (4/12/2016)

# 6
# *Life Lived Well*

In the previous chapters, we noted the ethical rules that are divided into four pillars (4Ps). The reasoning within these pillars is briefly summarized in this way:

- Prohibited Acts: Stay far away from the brink.
- Prescriptions: Find the right solution to problems encountered along the way.
- Priorities: Concentrate on the goal. "Keep your eyes on the ball."
- Providence and Grace: You need outside help, particularly God's help. Seek it. Treasure it.

This chapter presents several additional ethical considerations.

## 6.1 Precedence among the Rules

In practical moral decisions, a single act may involve more than one ethical rule and different rules may mean conflicting advice. In that case we a need to take into account the precedence among the rules.

Violation of prohibitions can completely destroy the hope to reach the big goal. Therefore the prohibitions always have precedence over all other rules (see intrinsic evil in Chapter 3).

The first question to ask about an act is: Is the act prohibited? If it is, the act is not moral and should not be considered any further. All false solutions to a moral problem that violate explicit prohibitions, like mercy killing or mercy lying, are grave ethical distortions. Note that in the encounter with the rich young man, Jesus brings up the prohibitions first and only after that, he speaks about other moral rules (Mt 19:17).

The First Commandment requires us to choose the Kingdom of God over all competing earthly goods, hence the second question is: Can this act be sanctified, or does it lead me away from God? If it does, it should not be considered.

Next question is based on prescriptions and there are priorities among them. Some are more conducive to reaching the Kingdom of God and therefore take precedence over other lesser ones. Merciful justice is a particularly important prescription in this respect. (Mt 25:31-46). However, note that merciful justice requires rationality, humility, and fortitude. It cannot contradict these fundamental virtues and also cannot contradict basic moral prohibitions as noted earlier.

Our own salvation has precedence over everything else, so we should ask: How much of a threat to our salvation should we take on behalf of others, to rescue somebody who is imperiled? That is, how much moral danger should we voluntarily place ourselves in to help save someone? The parable of the wise and foolish virgins is a cautionary tale that explains that there is a limit (Mt 25:1-3).

Sometimes we have to humbly acknowledge that certain things are beyond our reach. For example, it would be wrong to join a destructive cult or a false religion with the idea of helping to convert their members from within, or to marry a morally depraved person so that he or she might be brought to God. These choices would not be acts of mercy, but acts of self-destructive foolishness and pride.

## 6.2 Additional Prescriptions

Several New Testament prescriptions require more elaborate thinking than simply seeking Aristotelian balance between defect and excess. Consider these two examples.

### Sabbath Rest

Resting on the Sabbath is a prescription that has its origin in the Old Testament (Ex 20:8-11). Sabbath rest allows us to replenish our energy and reaffirm our dignity as free people. The New Testament reaffirms Sabbath rest (Heb 4:9). However, Jesus demonstrated that handling emergencies or performing acts of mercy take precedence over Sabbath rest:

> One Sabbath, when he went to dine at the house of a ruler of the Pharisees, they were watching him carefully. And behold, there was a man before him who had dropsy. And Jesus responded to the lawyers and Pharisees, saying, "Is it lawful to heal on the Sabbath, or not?" But they remained silent. Then he took him and healed him and sent him away. And he said to them, "Which of you, having a son or an ox that has fallen into a well on a Sabbath day, will not immediately pull him out?" (Lk 14:1-6)

The Pharisees believed that there is a total prohibition against work on the Sabbath and applied "stay far away from the brink" type of reasoning. They assembled lists of activities they thought were prohibited on the Sabbath and they consequently turned the Sabbath into an excess of oppressive and unreasonable restrictions. Jesus puts the Sabbath into proper perspective: "Then he said to them, 'The Sabbath was made for man, not man for the Sabbath'" (Mk 2:27).

### Honor Your Father and Mother

There is a school in modern psychology that blames parents for all ills in the lives of their children. This thinking is unjust and ungrateful towards parents. Our parents brought us into the world and that requires gratitude. Even if our parents have failed us in a significant way, we must forgive, as lack of forgiveness damages the people who harbor it.

The prescription "Honor Your Father and Mother" tells us how to deal with parents, but it has to be lived differently in different phases of human life. The New Testament contains the following narrative that illustrates how dependent children should behave:

> *Now his parents went to Jerusalem every year at the feast of the Passover. And when he was twelve years old, they went up according to custom; and when the feast was ended, as they were returning, the boy Jesus stayed behind in Jerusalem. His parents did not know it, but supposing him to be in the company they went a day's journey, and they sought him among their kinsfolk and acquaintances; and when they did not find him, they returned to Jerusalem, seeking him.*
>
> *After three days they found him in the temple, sitting among the teachers, listening to them and asking them questions; and all who heard him were amazed at his understanding and his answers. And when they saw him they were astonished; and his mother said to him, "Son, why have you treated us so? Behold, your father and I have been looking for you anxiously." And he said to them, "How is it that you sought me? Did you not know that I must be in my Father's house?" And they did not understand the saying which he spoke to them. And he went down with them and came to Nazareth, and was obedient to them; and his mother kept all these things in her heart. (Lk 2:41-51)*

We could speculate that if Jesus had stayed in the temple and studied there, he would have become a noted scripture scholar and that would have opened up opportunities at the start of his public ministry. That prospect was lost by his return to Nazareth. When Jesus started his public ministry, he was treated as an outsider from Galilee which limited his early audience (Jn 7:52). From a purely human perspective, the return to Nazareth was a setback. Nevertheless, Jesus obeyed his earthly parents, even with their limited understanding of his divine mission (Lk 2:51). By his example, he showed that dependent children are to obey their parents.

However when children reach independence, they have to fulfill God's plan in their lives, even if it contradicts their parents' wishes. This is implied by another event from the Gospels:

> *Then his mother and his brothers came to him, but they could not reach him for the crowd. And he was told, "Your mother and your brothers are standing outside, desiring to see you." But he said to them, "My mother and my brothers are those who hear the word of God and do it." (Lk 8:19-21)*

In the last phase of human life, parents are old and are no longer able to care for themselves. There is a duty of their children to step in and take care of them. Jesus again provides inspiration:

> *But standing by the cross of Jesus were his mother, and his mother's sister, Mary the wife of Clopas, and Mary Magdalene. When Jesus saw his mother, and the disciple whom he loved standing near, he said to his mother, "Woman, behold, your son!" Then he said to the disciple, "Behold, your mother!" And from that hour the disciple took her to his own home. (Jn 19:25-27)*

This is a scene of desolation where Jesus is stripped of his earthly possessions and crucified. His mother is a widow and her only son is approaching death. All of the apostles had fled except for John, who stayed with Jesus. In this situation, Jesus uses the last earthly asset he still has—influence with his disciple John—and directs John to take care of his mother in her old age. Jesus thereby gives us an example on how to honor our father and mother—within our means—at the end of our parents' lives.

## 6.3  Answers to Some Simplistic Ethical Theories

Some popular ethical theories of today, such as those noted below, focus on a single issue. But often the advice is slanted towards excess, similar to the Pharisees' misunderstanding of the Sabbath. The resulting ethical guidance is distorted and dangerous to the people who live by it. This section presents several of these theories.

### Freedom

Authentic freedom is an indispensable component of living a moral life, because ethical choices are impossible without the ability to make free decisions. Freedom is one of the blessings that must not be squandered: "You were bought with a price; do not become slaves of men" (1 Cor 7:23). Note that the rich young man decides that the demands of the full New Testament Ethics are too much for him. He walks away freely and Jesus doesn't try to stop him (Mt 19:22).

However, some people simplistically reduce freedom to a right to do whatever they momentarily please, but freedom is better understood as an opportunity to pursue things that are good for us. That includes the pursuit of big goals. As mentioned earlier, big goals can be reached only by following the rules.

New Testament ethical rules play an analogous role. While they restrict certain acts, they open new possibilities that truly benefit us: "Live as free men," St. Peter exhorts, "yet without using your freedom as a pretext for evil; but live as servants of God" (1 Pet 2:16).

While authentic freedom is essential for moral life, it is not an end in itself. New Testament prohibitions limit simplistically understood freedom, but they give us the freedom to seek the Kingdom of God.

### Tolerance

We often encounter behaviors or traits in others that we find bothersome. The virtue of tolerance helps us to disregard misleading feelings or spurious generalizations. Synonyms or closely related virtues are "broadmindedness," "acceptance," and "forbearance."

Tolerance is the sweet spot between two extremes. The deficiency is called *intolerance* and has various manifestations that include "bigotry," "prejudice," or "bias." The other extreme of excess is "whitewashing," "concealing," "glossing over," or "willful blindness."

Jesus condemns the careless passing of judgment on others: "Judge not, that you be not judged" (Mt 7:1). However St. Paul disapproves the excess of willful blindness and counsels reproof and correction if situation calls for it (2 Tim 3:16). He also cautions us against whitewashing and approving evil (Rom 1:32), or participate in other people's sins (Eph 5:11; 1 Tim 5:22). If necessary, he even counsels us to disassociate ourselves from unrepentant evildoers and false leaders: "Do not be deceived: Bad company ruins good morals" (1 Cor 15:33; see also 2 Cor 6:17; Rom 16:17; 1 Cor 5:9-11; 2 Thess 3:14).

Modern society often proclaims tolerance as a great virtue, but publicly practices an excess with serious blind spots. For example, favored individuals or groups are whitewashed, while legitimate disapproval of their deficiencies is misrepresented as a form of intolerance. This distorted version of tolerance is no longer a virtue. Instead, it is an unjust double standard that bestows undeserved favors on some and deals severely with others.

## Relativism

While morally significant acts are the focus of the New Testament Ethics, many acts are morally neutral. For example, it does not ethically matter whether we eat boiled or scrambled eggs for breakfast, or whether we wear brown or black socks. Even the acts that have a large impact on our life can be morally neutral, like choosing one's profession or choosing a place to live.

However moral relativism does not make a distinction between morally neutral and morally significant acts. Instead, it reacts to all acts as if they are morally neutral. Note how ridiculous relativism is in the context of big goals where one might say, "I like to drive on left side of the road," or "I like to have a couple of alcoholic drinks before I drive." Should these "values" be accepted with understanding?

On the opposite extreme is moralistic excess, which imposes restrictions where none are needed and thus infringes on people's freedom.

The New Testament Ethics is situated in the sweet spot between the extremes of moral relativism and moralistic excess. It consists of rules for morally significant acts and is completely open in morally neutral ones. It is based on the understanding that for morally significant acts, there is always legitimate authority that sets rules, and we must submit to that authority to achieve our goal. For the road trip to Chicago, that authority is the state legislature that establishes the traffic rules. For the studies that lead to a degree, it is the university that creates the academic rules. For seeking the Kingdom of God, God establishes the rules.

The Bible illustrates the danger of relativism: "Woe to those who call evil good and good evil, who put darkness for light and light for darkness, who put bitter for sweet and sweet for bitter!" (Is 5:20).

## Proportionalism

We weigh costs and benefits when we go shopping, that is, we compare the cost (the price in dollars) against the benefit of the goods we may want to buy. If we conclude that the cost/benefit is reasonable, we buy. This cost/benefit analysis is fine in morally good or neutral acts and it is a part of the virtue of rationality.

Proportionalism however is an excess, a variant of consequentialism that was mentioned earlier, and leads a person to focus on the proportion between the good and bad effects, justifying immoral acts by the "greater good" or "lesser evil." Such misguided moral calculus is objectively immoral and can result in grave injustices, as the following example shows:

*If we let him go on thus, every one will believe in him, and the Romans will come and destroy both our holy place and our nation. But one of them, Caiaphas, who was high priest that year, said to them, "You know nothing at all; you do not understand that it is expedient for you that one man should die for the people, and that the whole nation should not perish."* (Jn 11:48-50)

This crude proportionalistic reasoning by Caiaphas weighed the death of one man (cost) against the survival of a whole nation (benefit) and considered the resulting outcome to be lesser evil. However, his calculus crossed into an intrinsic evil, because sentencing an innocent man to death is murder, which cannot be justified by any expected benefit.

History shows how wrong Caiaphas' calculus was. There was no real threat from the Romans at that time that would be mollified by the death of Jesus, as the Romans only reluctantly participated in his execution (Mt 27:24). The catastrophe that troubled Caiaphas happened several decades later. During the First Jewish-Roman War, the mighty Roman army mercilessly crushed the Jewish revolt. The temple, the center of Jewish life, was destroyed, and a huge humanitarian catastrophe unfolded. The only real consequence of Caiaphas' flawed reasoning was the murder of an innocent victim.

Proportionalism is often employed by the powerful who assign a higher weight to their own interests vs. the interests of others. It gives them an excuse for injustices based on the "greater good" or "lesser evil."

## 6.4 Human Traits

Besides individual human acts that have been studied in this book, there are persistent human traits that stay with us throughout our lives. They are discussed in the rest of this chapter.

### Habits

Habits are regularly repeated behaviors. To follow an ingrained habit is easy, while the behavior that contradicts that habit can be hard. A Czech proverb characterizes a habit as a "shirt made of iron."

When trying to live a good life, good habits are a great help while bad habits are a grave hindrance. Habitual obeying traffic rules makes Hannah's trip to Chicago safer, while habitual speeding increases the likelihood of an accident or getting a traffic ticket. Good study habits improve Jacob's chances of earning a college degree, while bad habits, like procrastination, make it less likely.

A persistent struggle to live according to the New Testament will form good habits, and these habits will make our future struggles easier. The first step towards developing a good habit is to think about it and give assent to it in our mind. That will make right decisions easier when the time to act comes: "Finally, brethren, whatever is true, whatever is honorable, whatever is just, whatever is pure, whatever is lovely, whatever is gracious, if there is any excellence, if there is anything worthy of praise, think about these things" (Phil 4:8).

Our "moral character" is the sum of all our habits. It is the best predictor of how we will act in the future. Occasionally people act "out of character," in both positive or negative ways, but that is relatively infrequent.

Both virtuous acts and virtuous habits are commonly called "virtues."

## Conscience

Conscience is an "inner voice" that indicts our acts or excuses them. St. Paul explains conscience in this way: "When Gentiles who have not the law do by nature what the law requires, they are a law unto themselves, even though they do not have the law. They show that what the law requires is written on their hearts, while their conscience also bears witness and their conflicting thoughts accuse or perhaps excuse them" (Rom 2:14-15). It means that even people who do not follow the New Testament Ethics ("Gentiles") still know deep down ("written on their heart") the New Testament rules ("the law") and their own conscience judges their acts accordingly.

Since each person has a moral conscience, it is part of God's providence. An accusing conscience fosters inner turmoil, but an affirming conscience cultivates inner peace. In popular culture, people some-times allude to their conscience when they say, "I have to (or I can-not) do this, so that I can look at myself in the mirror."

Our conscience not only judges past actions, but also reminds us of obligations and also guides our future acts. However, our con-science can make an error and misjudge an act. Good acts still remain good acts, even when misjudged by conscience, and bad acts still remain bad acts.

Humans have other dispositions that can compete with conscience. Jesus talked about these negative dispositions as originating from "the heart." He said: "From within people, from their hearts, come evil thoughts, unchastity, theft, murder, adultery, greed, malice, deceit, licentiousness, envy, blasphemy, arrogance, folly. All these evils come from within and they defile" (Mk 7:21-23).

In exercising our free will, we have to decide which dispositions we are going to follow. There are saints who have rejected selfishness and succeeded to follow their conscience in an exemplary way. On the opposite extreme, malevolent people have largely extinguished their conscience and are spreading destruction around them, moti-vated by their malignant selfishness.

Every act that conforms to New Testament Ethics sharpens our conscience while every act that contradicts New Testament, dulls it. St. Paul calls a well-formed conscience a "good conscience" (1 Tim 1:5) or a "clear conscience" (2 Tim 1:3).

## Work and its Fruits

The First Commandment mandates that we love God over everyone and everything that this world can offer, but it would be wrong to conclude that it advocates the neglect of the persons and things of this world. To the contrary; many passages of the New Testament approvingly note the work that people do to improve the world. There are the shepherds tending their sheep (Lk 2:8), the sower sowing his seed (Lk 8:5), fishermen minding their boats and fishing nets (Jn 21: 5), the winegrower managing his vineyard (Mk 12:1), the virgins getting oil for the lamps (Mt 25:5) and a father sending his sons to go to work in his vineyard (Mk 21:28). Jesus practiced carpentry most of his adult life (Mk 6:3). These references to work are scattered through the New Testament to show that work that enhances the world is an essential part of our lives.

In Chapter 4, we noted that both earthly concerns and the First Commandment can be reconciled by offering everything, including work and its results, to God. St. Paul advises "rendering service with a good will as to the Lord and not to men" (Eph 6:7). Jesus also counsels us to finish our projects, not abandon them midstream (Lk 14:29-30). As stated earlier, the First Commandment is not an excuse for sloppiness, laziness, daydreaming or absentmindedness. On the contrary, taking good care of earthly things is part of our path to the Kingdom of God.

One of the benefits of work is that it teaches us the whole range of virtues. We learn not only industriousness, but also patience when the results are slow in coming, fortitude and ambition when there is uncertainty or opposition, and trust and honesty when dealing with other people.

The same virtues also apply to the journey towards the Kingdom of God. For example, several apostles were originally fishermen on the Sea of Galilee (Mk 1:16–20). Later they became "fishers of men" and we can infer that they brought to their new mission the virtues they learned in their trade as fishermen: proactive caring for their boats and nets combined with the reactive virtues of patience and endurance while fishing on the sea. No doubt, their professional experiences prepared them to deal with both successes and failures in their apostolate.

Another example is the apostle Matthew, a well-educated tax collector who became the author of one of the Gospels (Mt 9:9-13). From these and other examples, we can conclude that human work is a training ground of virtues that are also needed for the Kingdom of God.

## Repentant Sinner

At the end of our life, God will judge our entire life. What counts at the moment of our death counts forever and what does not count at the moment of death does not count at all. It pays to prepare for that monumental culmination. The Gospels contain numerous references to this final accounting, for example the parable of the talents (Mt 25:14- 30), parable of the rich man and Lazarus (Lk 16:19- 31), and the parable of the rich fool (Lk 12:13-31).

Semester finals, where students demonstrate what they learned in the entire course, can be used as an analogy. However, there is one important difference: Finals are scheduled well in advance, which allows students to cram for their exams a day or two before. In contrast, death and our judgment can come unexpectedly at any moment and this should create in us a sense of urgency. Jesus tells us to be watchful:

> Take heed, watch and pray; for you do not know when the time will come. It is like a man going on a journey, when he leaves home and puts his servants in charge, each with his work, and commands the doorkeeper to be on the watch. Watch therefore— for you do not know when the master of the house will come, in the evening, or at midnight, or at cockcrow, or in the morning— lest he come suddenly and find you asleep. And what I say to you I say to all: Watch! (Mk 13:33-37)

Running out the clock may be a good strategy for a winning team in American football, but it is a poor strategy for attaining the Kingdom of God. The cautionary story of the foolish virgins who failed to use their available time shows the eternal costs of gross negligence in our relationship with God (Mt 25:1-13).

We already mentioned the conversion that leads to the acceptance of faith, like the one experienced by St. Paul (Acts 9:3–19). However, repentance and conversion are a continuing process. In the analogy of the car trip, whenever Hannah is driving in the wrong direction, she has to acknowledge the problem, change her course, and make up for the lost miles.

Similarly, on the road towards the Kingdom of God we have to acknowledge our past wrongs, change and do penance. Jesus encourages this continuous repentance: "But I have this against you, that you have abandoned the love you had at first. Remember then from what you have fallen, repent and do the works you did at first. If not, I will come to you and remove your lampstand from its place, unless you repent" (Rev 2:4-5). In addition, "Those whom I love, I reprove and chasten; so be zealous and repent" (Rev 3:19).

Unforgiving systems like some human courts often even use repentance as evidence of wrongdoing, which leads to denial, cover-up and other moral pathologies. In contrast, Jesus offers a liberating system based on mercy and forgiveness. It offers a new beginning through repentance, allowing us to leave our past sins behind and pursue the Kingdom of God with renewed freedom.

Repentance is such an important factor that a follower of the New Testament Ethics is sometimes identified as a "repentant sinner." The repentant sinner mindset encourages humility and prayer rather than combative fanaticism. "Repent therefore, and turn again," St. Peter exhorts us, "that your sins may be blotted out, that times of refreshing may come from the presence of the Lord" (Acts 3:19).

## Human Flourishing

Jesus reminds us that the life he offers us is characterized by love: "He who has my commandments and keeps them, he it is who loves me; and he who loves me will be loved by my Father, and I will love him and manifest myself to him" (Jn 14:21). Jesus elaborates further: "If you keep my commandments, you will abide in my love, just as I have kept my Father's commandments and abide in his love" (Jn 15:10).

Jesus also tells us to perceive ourselves as *children of God*, basking in His generosity and love (Mt 7:11). In the prayer he taught us, he teaches us to address God as our father (Mt 6:9). This noble pedigree should give us self-esteem and hope that we need for our struggles.

The result of embracing New Testament Ethics is a balanced personality and a life lived well, which is sometimes called a holy life or the *life of a saint*. The ancient Greeks dreamed of a life lived well, although they restricted it to earthly happiness, because the idea of eternal happiness was alien to them. They called their goal *eudaimonia*, translated as "happiness" or "human flourishing." It was a weak anticipation of the Kingdom of God, because the ancient Greeks pursued their goal without the help of grace.

Yet the ancient Greeks noticed this asymmetry: "... it is possible to fail in many ways, while to succeed is possible only in one way" (Aristotle). The same is true when seeking the Kingdom of God. Jesus uses the "narrow gate" analogy: "Enter by the narrow gate; for the gate is wide and the way is easy, that leads to destruction, and those who enter by it are many. For the gate is narrow and the way is hard, that leads to life, and those who find it are few" (Mt 7:13-14).

The example of Hannah's trip to Chicago illustrated many aspects of pursuing the big goal, but there is an important difference. It is relatively easy to reach Chicago and the great majority of people who undertake this trip succeed. In comparison, it is much harder to reach Kingdom of God and "those who find it are few" (Mt 7:14). However, so we don't get discouraged, St. John offers a vision of people who have successfully reached the Kingdom of God. They are from every nation and tribe and they are so many that nobody can count them (Rev 7:9). This vision tells us that although there are many difficulties on the way, Kingdom of God is reachable and countless number of people will find it.

## 6.5 Further Study

Pope St. John Paul II criticizes proportionalism and the notions of "lesser evil" and "greater good" that often camouflage intrinsic evil (VS 75-81). A better alternative to proportionalism is the principle of the double effect. It addresses the morality of acts that may have both good and bad results, but takes precautions against slipping into intrinsic evil, see *Double-effect Reasoning* (Cavanaugh, 2006).

*Catechism of the Catholic Church* teaches that we have a responsibility for the sins committed by others when we cooperate in those transgressions:

- by participating directly and voluntarily in them;
- by ordering, advising, praising, or approving them;
- by not disclosing or not hindering them when we have an obligation to do so;
- by protecting evil-doers (CCC 1868).

Correct understanding of conscience is an important theological and ethical issue (CCC 1776-1802, VS 54-64). Work and its role in human life is discussed in *Friends of God* (Escriva, 1981).

The New Testament in general speaks about individual acts rather than habits. However acts collectively form habits, either morally good or bad ones, which in turn help or hinder seeking our goals. There are numerous studies on how to form good habits and overcome bad ones. Some publications study how long it takes to form habits. One study found that it takes anywhere from 18 to 254 days (Lally, Van Jaarsveld, Potts, & Wardle, 2010).

"Project Happiness" tries to recreate the ancient Greek project of eudaimonia, however it misses the need of providence and grace (McGregor & Little, 1998; Rubin, 2010). This omission casts serious doubt on this project.

Some people who are advanced in their spiritual journey, experience the feeling of being abandoned by God. It may be short or long, and it is called "the dark Night of the Soul." It is a purging of attachments to earthly things and can be a major step towards the freedom of the Kingdom of God, but it involves suffering. It was humanly experienced by Jesus on the cross (Mt 27:46) and it is described in Psalm 22 (Stimson, 2015).

**Questions for Reflection or Group Discussion**

1. What was wrong with the Pharisees' reasoning about Sabbath rest?

2. Is considering possible costs and benefits always right? Always wrong?

3. What is the role of freedom in human life?

4. What is the error of relativism?

5. How does conscience affect our acts?

6. Several of the apostles were fishermen by their trade. How can the training of your profession be used in service of the First Commandment?

## References

Aristotle. *Nicomachean Ethics*. In J. L. Ackrill (Ed.), *A New Aristotle Reader* (pp. 363 - 478). Princeton, N.J.: Princeton University Press.

Cavanaugh, T. A. (2006). *Double-Effect Reasoning: Doing Good and Avoiding Evil*: Oxford University Press.

Escriva, J. (1981). *Friends of God: Homilies*: Scepter Publishers.

Lally, P., Van Jaarsveld, C. H., Potts, H. W., & Wardle, J. (2010). *How are Habits Formed: Modelling habit formation in the real world.* European Journal of Social Psychology, 40(6), 998-1009.

McGregor, I., & Little, B. R. (1998). *Personal Projects, Happiness, and Meaning: on Doing Well and Being Yourself.* Journal of personality and social psychology, 74(2), 494.

Rubin, G. C. (2010). *The Happiness Project*: HarperPaperbacks.

Stimson, E. (2015). *Understanding the 'dark night of the soul'.* Our Sunday Visitor. https://www.osv.com/osvnewsweekly/byissue/article/tabid/735/artmid/13636/articleid/17512/understanding-the-%E2%80%98dark-night-of-the-soul%E2%80%99-.aspx?ref=top10 (1/16/2016)

# 7
# *In the World*

Besides the prescriptions that we covered so far, the New Testament also contains specific prescriptions on how to conduct ourselves in a society and the world. They are summarized in this final chapter.

## 7.1 Neighbors and Nearest Neighbors

We already mentioned that the New Testament requires treating the whole human race as neighbors (Lk 10:36–37). However in our lives, we directly interact with only a limited number of people, our "nearest neighbors." These are people we personally know and who know us. They are a litmus test for the seriousness of our love of our neighbor. There is nothing more un-Christian than expressing lofty concerns for the far-away people, while mistreating the people with whom we directly interact.

### Family

Our nuclear family members are our most intimate neighbors. St. Paul presents prescriptions on how we should interact with each other:

> *Wives, be subject to your husbands, as to the Lord. For the husband is the head of the wife as Christ is the head of the church, his body,*

*and is himself its Savior. As the church is subject to Christ, so let wives also be subject in everything to their husbands. Husbands, love your wives, as Christ loved the church and gave himself up for her, that he might sanctify her, having cleansed her by the washing of water with the word, that he might present the church to himself in splendor, without spot or wrinkle or any such thing, that she might be holy and without blemish. Even so husbands should love their wives as their own bodies. He who loves his wife loves himself. For no man ever hates his own flesh, but nourishes and cherishes it, as Christ does the church, because we are members of his body.*

*"For this reason a man shall leave his father and mother and be joined to his wife, and the two shall become one flesh." This mystery is a profound one, and I am saying that it refers to Christ and the church; however, let each one of you love his wife as himself, and let the wife see that she respects her husband. Children, obey your parents in the Lord, for this is right. "Honor your father and mother" (this is the first commandment with a promise), "that it may be well with you and that you may live long on the earth." Fathers, do not provoke your children to anger, but bring them up in the discipline and instruction of the Lord. (Eph 5:22-6:4)*

This passage contains precepts for interactions between husbands, wives and children. They are variants of the prescriptions that were already mentioned earlier, but they acquire a particular urgency within a family.

St. Paul teaches that a husband is called to be a head of his family and that headship has to be based on an emulation of Christ's role in the church (Eph 5:22). Like Christ, the husband must give priority to his nuclear family over other ties, even those with his own human parents (Eph 5:31) and love his wife as himself (Eph 5:33). He must be ready to lay down his life for his family as Christ did for the Church (Eph 5:25). Such heroic love helps his wife to be "without spot or wrinkle or any such thing" and "holy and without blemish" (Eph 5:26-29).

St. Paul also teaches that in turn, a wife should help her husband to fulfil his role by respecting him (Eph 5:32) and by living heroically the virtue of meekness, called in this passage by a synonym "be subject to" (Eph 5:22, 24). The passage also reminds children to honor their parents. However, it also exhorts fathers not to provoke children to anger and to bring them up well (Eph 6:1-4).

Living virtues in the family setting is challenging and St. Paul himself wonders about the teaching he is espousing: "This mystery is a profound one . . ." (Eph 5:32). We can speculate that while all virtues are essential for harmony in family, love of the wife is singled out for husbands because it is especially important and challenging, and meekness is especially important and challenging for wives.

Strong families are much needed in our society in which the nuclear family is under attack from widespread divorce, cohabitation of unmarried couples, growing unwed birth rate and even redefinition of the fundamental concept of marriage.

## Friendship

Friendship is a loving relationship with another person. It teaches many virtues, including generosity, magnanimity and tolerance. Desire of friendship is one of the natural desires and lack of friendship, loneliness, can be a heavy burden (Cacioppo & Patrick, 2008). Jesus refers to His followers as friends:

> This is my commandment, that you love one another as I have loved you. Greater love has no man than this, that a man lay down his life for his friends. You are my friends if you do what I command you. No longer do I call you servants, for the servant does not know what his master is doing; but I have called you friends, for all that I have heard from my Father I have made known to you. You did not choose me, but I chose you and appointed you that you should go and bear fruit and that your fruit should abide; so that whatever you ask the Father in my name, he may give it to you. This I command you, to love one another. (Jn 15:12-17)

St. Paul provides advice on friendship: "Therefore encourage one another and build one another up, just as you are doing" (1 Thess

5:11). That means to strengthen a friend's strong traits and gently leading them away from their bad ones. He also exemplifies friendship in his letters to his friends Titus, Timothy, and Philemon. These letters are full of St. Paul's concerns and advice as to how to deal with various situations.

St. Peter provides further advice: "Above all hold unfailing your love for one another, since love covers a multitude of sins. Practice hospitality ungrudgingly to one another. As each has received a gift, employ it for one another, as good stewards of God's varied grace" (1 Pet 4:8-10).

## Disapproval from Others

The pursuit of big goals, unfortunately, does not meet with universal approval. While some people show genuine admiration, other people look at the quest for such goals with doubt or even scorn. Many people who have studied for an advanced degree, raised a large family or started a business, can attest that there are people who view their pursuits with skepticism and even contempt.

The quest for the Kingdom of God is no exception, as St. Paul reminds us: "[B]ut we preach Christ crucified, a stumbling block to Jews and folly to Gentiles" (1Cor 1:23). During a confrontation, this contempt can escalate into hatred:

> *Again he entered the synagogue, and a man was there who had a withered hand. And they watched him, to see whether he would heal him on the sabbath, so that they might accuse him. And he said to the man who had the withered hand, "Come here." And he said to them, "Is it lawful on the sabbath to do good or to do harm, to save life or to kill?" But they were silent. And he looked around at them with anger, grieved at their hardness of heart, and said to the man, "Stretch out your hand." He stretched it out, and his hand was restored. The Pharisees went out, and immediately held counsel with the Herodians against him, how to destroy him. (Mk 3:1-6)*

In this confrontation, the people without goodwill disregarded the miracle that was happening in front of their own eyes. Instead, they zoomed in on a distorted issue of the Sabbath rest and agreed on an outrageously hostile response (Mk 3:6). They demonstrated how the world often cannot distinguish virtue from vice.

The disapproval can even invade our family and Jesus warns of the strife this can cause: "For I have come to set a man against his father, and a daughter against her mother, and a daughter-in-law against her mother-in-law; and a man's foes will be those of his own household" (Mt 10:34-37).

When operating in a hostile environment, rational assessment of a situation and caution is necessary: "Do not give dogs what is holy; and do not throw your pearls before swine, lest they trample them under foot and turn to attack you" (Mt 7:6).

In addition, liars can portray Jesus and his followers as a threat: "And in the synagogue there was a man who had the spirit of an unclean demon; and he cried out with a loud voice, Ah! What have you to do with us, Jesus of Nazareth? Have you come to destroy us? I know who you are, the Holy One of God" (Lk 4:33-34).

## Betrayal

Judas was one of the apostles, the inner circle of Jesus throughout his public ministry. His story is so well-known that "thirty pieces of silver" became and remains a notorious metaphor for betrayal:

> *Then one of the twelve, who was called Judas Iscariot, went to the chief priests and said, "What will you give me if I deliver him to you?" And they paid him thirty pieces of silver. And from that moment he sought an opportunity to betray him. (Mt 26:14-16)*

Betrayal by a friend or a family member can be one of the most painful of human experiences. Fidelity to the First Commandment is our primary defense; it reminds us to love God over everyone and everything else and God will never betray us.

## 7.2 State and Culture

Besides interactions with our nearest neighbors, we also live in the larger community. That larger community has a certain prevailing culture and is organized as a state and its various units. Some of the New Testament prescriptions address our interactions with this larger community.

### State

The state is an organized political community that plays a unique role by providing its citizens and other residents with security and justice. The New Testament authors repeatedly exhort us to be loyal citizens of the state (Rom 13:1, 5; 1 Pet 2:13, 1 Pet 2:17). However, loyalty to the state must not encroach on our relationship with God:

> *Then the Pharisees went and took counsel how to entangle him in his talk. And they sent their disciples to him, along with the Herodians, saying, "Teacher, we know that you are true, and teach the way of God truthfully, and care for no man; for you do not regard the position of men. Tell us, then, what you think. Is it lawful to pay taxes to Caesar, or not?" But Jesus, aware of their malice, said, "Why put me to the test, you hypocrites? Show me the money for the tax." And they brought him a coin. And Jesus said to them, "Whose likeness and inscription is this?" They said, "Caesar's." Then he said to them, "Render therefore to Caesar the things that are Caesar's, and to God the things that are God's." (Mt 22:15-21)*

When putting things in perspective, our association with a state will end when we move or die. But our relationship with God is eternal:

> *Our commonwealth is in heaven, and from it we await a Savior, the Lord Jesus Christ, who will change our lowly body to be like his glorious body, by the power which enables him even to subject all things to himself. (Phil 3:20-21)*

## Culture

The culture of a society includes prevailing knowledge, beliefs, art, morals, laws and customs. It is never fully aligned to the demands of the New Testament.

St. Paul stresses that in all circumstances we should exercise social responsibility (1 Tim 2:8-15; 5:1-2, 9-14; 6:1-2) and look not only to our own interests, but also to the interests of others (Phil 2:4). We also should not worry excessively about injustices in the world that we cannot do anything about. Instead, Jesus tells us to concentrate on our own behavior: "... there is nothing outside a man which by going into him can defile him; but the things which come out of a man are what defile him" (Mk 7:15). In cases of a grave and persistent sin in the society, justice is ultimately in the hands of God:

> *Just as the weeds are gathered and burned with fire, so will it be at the close of the age. The Son of man will send his angels, and they will gather out of his kingdom all causes of sin and all evildoers, and throw them into the furnace of fire; there men will weep and gnash their teeth. Then the righteous will shine like the sun in the kingdom of their Father. (Mt 13:40-43)*

## Persecution

Many societies persecute Christians and one of the Beatitudes indicates soberly that persecution is part and parcel of seeking the Kingdom of God (Mt 5:10-12). In this context, St. Peter calls for fortitude: "But even if you do suffer for righteousness' sake, you will be blessed. Have no fear of them, nor be troubled" (1 Pet 3:14).

Because of the negative attitude towards Jesus and his Church in many societies, it requires courage to acknowledge our faith publicly. Jesus says there is ultimately a heavenly reward for doing this: "So every one who acknowledges me before men, I also will acknowledge before my Father who is in heaven; but whoever denies me before men, I also will deny before my Father who is in heaven" (Mt 10: 32-33).

Jesus describes the travails that may await a true disciple of his, and yet he reassures us that God's grace will help us to endure our trials:

*Behold, I send you out as sheep in the midst of wolves; so be wise as serpents and innocent as doves. Beware of men; for they will deliver you up to councils, and flog you in their synagogues, .and you will be dragged before governors and kings for my sake, to bear testimony before them and the Gentiles. When they deliver you up, do not be anxious how you are to speak or what you are to say; for what you are to say will be given to you in that hour; for it is not you who speak, but the Spirit of your Father speaking through you.*

*Brother will deliver up brother to death, and the father his child, and children will rise against parents and have them put to death; and you will be hated by all for my name's sake. But he who endures to the end will be saved. When they persecute you in one town, flee to the next; for truly, I say to you, you will not have gone through all the towns of Israel, before the Son of man comes. "A disciple is not above his teacher, nor a servant above his master; it is enough for the disciple to be like his teacher, and the servant like his master. If they have called the master of the house Beelzebub, how much more will they malign those of his household. (Mt 10:16-25)*

### Social Leaven

There are many blueprints on how to organize society. Note that Jesus announced his social program early in his ministry, when he returned to preach in Nazareth:

*The Spirit of the Lord is upon me, because he has anointed me to preach good news to the poor. He has sent me to proclaim release to the captives and recovering of sight to the blind, to set at liberty those who are oppressed. (Lk 4:18)*

This ambitious social program originates in the Old Testament (Is

61:1-2) and it continues with Jesus and his Church. The "captives" include people oppressed by an unjust social order, sinners who cannot break their bad habits and sufferers wounded by the sins of the others. Their release is going to be accomplished by the cumulative impact of many individual acts, done by people who sincerely seek the Kingdom of God.

These acts benefit society in many subtle ways, without much fanfare and without loud proclamations: ". . . The kingdom of heaven is like leaven which a woman took and hid in three measures of flour, till it was all leavened" (Mt 13:33). The social benefit of individual Christian action is sometimes so gradual that it is hard to perceive, and can be called the "invisible hand of God."

> ▪ **Benefits for All**
>
> Respect for traffic rules benefits not only the individual traveler but everybody on the road. Each traveler who observes these rules helps traffic move smoothly and also helps decrease the number of road accidents, which, in turn, makes travel more pleasant for everyone. On the other hand, Hannah's freedom to travel to Chicago can be threatened not only by someone who might prohibit that trip, but also by anarchy on the road, where drivers do as they please and thus threaten the well-being of everybody.

Both individual and social benefits offered by the Kingdom of God grow almost imperceptibly, undeterred by adverse circumstances. There is the growth of an individual's inner peace that I encountered in Pavel Legerský, as I described earlier. Families, groups, towns, regions and/or entire societies that are leavened by the Kingdom of God, experience the gradual "release of captives" from confinements of all kinds. After death, the heavenly banquet awaits the followers of Jesus as their eternal gift and reward. To reach the Kingdom of God is the biggest goal of our lives. It should be towering over all our other goals and fulfills all desires that hide deep in our hearts.

## 7.3 Further Study

An essay by Scott Hahn explains ideal Christian marriage and contains additional references.

The social teachings of the Church address various aspects of Christians functioning in society. An example of a book that summarizes this topic is *Pillars of Catholic Social Teachings* (Roets, 1999). *Veritatis Splendor* also discusses these issues (VS 98-101).

### Questions for Reflection or Group Discussion

1. In what matters should we conform to society? In what matters should we not?

2. What is the basis for harmonious relations in a family?

3. How do friends build each other up? Give examples.

4. Why do some people disapprove of the pursuit of big goals?

5. How should we face betrayal?

6. How should Christians deal with the state?

7. How should Christians behave when being persecuted?

8. How does the Kingdom of God grow in society?

### References

Cacioppo, J. T., & Patrick, W. (2008). *Loneliness: Human Nature And The Need For Social Connection*: WW Norton & Company.

Hahn, S. *Christ And The Church: A Model For Marriage*. http://www3. nd.edu/~afreddos/courses/264/modmar.htm (12/5/2015).

Roets, P. J. (1999). *Pillars of Catholic Social Teachings: A Brief Social Catechism*: International Scholars Publications.

# Appendix: Additional Prescriptions

This Appendix explains several additional New Testament virtues, both proactive and reactive. Note that some of these virtues are very important for reaching the Kingdom of God.

## Honesty

One of the prohibitions covered in Chapter 1 disallows lying, but additional communication skills are needed beyond that. Honesty is one such skill and it directs how much to reveal to listeners.

It is based on the virtue of justice. Listeners have a right to certain information. Honesty is based on a respect of that right. It requires fortitude: An honest speaker sometimes presents inconvenient information or withholds information that the listeners demand. Synonyms for honesty include "sincerity," "authenticity," "genuineness," "openness," "discreetness," or "confidentiality."

The Aristotelian analysis leads us to seek the sweet spot between two extremes. The deficiency is *secretiveness*, also called "reticence" which leads to revealing too little. When combined with lying, it is called "dishonesty," "obfuscation," "insincerity," or "hypocrisy." The excess leads to disclosing too much and is called *indiscretion*, or "exhibitionism," or "shamelessness." The virtuous act lies between these two extremes. It leads to disclosing all information to which listeners are entitled, but keeping confidential the information to which they are not.

While honesty is an important virtue, unfortunately, it is under attack from many different directions because it is one of the greatly misunderstood virtues. For example, there are exhibitionists who delight in "baring it all" and are willing to publicize things that should stay hidden. Prime examples are various talk shows and "unauthorized" biographies. Excessive "honesty" is often presented as a false cure for hypocrisy but in reality it glorifies sin and is nothing else than shamelessness.

On the other extreme, expert manipulators develop techniques of insincerity, marketing products or political candidates without disclosing important information to which their listeners are entitled. This deception has become so widespread that it has affected our language. When we say somebody is "political," we often mean somebody is insincere.

Jesus gave examples of honesty when dealing with both his followers and detractors. When he was explaining his mission to his disciples, there was a great possibility of misunderstanding, but the message was something that the disciples needed to hear. Jesus was not "political" and this was the result:

> *Many of his disciples, when they heard it, said, "This is a hard saying; who can listen to it?" But Jesus, knowing in himself that his disciples murmured at it, said to them, "Do you take offense at this?" ... After this many of his disciples drew back and no longer went about with him. (John 6:60-66)*

However he also warned against indiscretion in the presence of a hostile audience that lacks good will (Mt 7:6).

## Kindness

The virtue of kindness is another quality that enhances our human interactions. It is based on love of our neighbor, as St. Paul reminds us: "Love is patient and *kind*; love does not envy or boast; it is not arrogant" (1 Cor 13:41). Synonyms and variants are "gentleness," "compassion," "benevolence," or "helpfulness."

Kindness is the Aristotelian sweet spot between the deficiency of *unkindness* or *rudeness*, and the excess of *niceness*, where the cowardly fear of the neighbor dominates and honesty is sacrificed in order to avoid conflict at any cost. Niceness is a very popular excess that is often confused with a virtue. "Fawning" or "obsequiousness" are other words used to describe niceness. Nice people do not give anybody any trouble. Doing that, they avoid trouble for themselves. For example, nice teachers do not flunk anybody, nice law enforcement officers do not give speeding tickets and nice speakers correctly evaluate what their listeners want to hear and then say exactly that. To say something "hurtful" is a grave trespass against niceness. To correct anybody's wrongdoing is another serious trespass in the world dominated by niceness.

Jesus systematically avoided this excess. There were many instances where he "told it like it is." Here's a good example:

> And he said, "Truly, I say to you, no prophet is acceptable in his own country. But in truth, I tell you, there were many widows in Israel in the days of Elijah, when the heaven was shut up three years and six months, when there came a great famine over all the land; and Elijah was sent to none of them but only to Zarephath, in the land of Sidon, to a woman who was a widow. And there were many lepers in Israel in the time of the prophet Elisha; and none of them was cleansed, but only Naaman the Syrian." When they heard this, all in the synagogue were filled with wrath. And they rose up and put him out of the city, and led him to the brow of the hill on which their city was built, that they might throw him down headlong. But passing through the midst of them he went away. (Lk 4:24-30)

In this event, Jesus told his listeners that during Israel's suffering, God sometimes bestowed His favor on foreigners. In other words, he told them that they do not have a monopoly on God's favor, and that God loves *all* people. This message was something they needed to hear. But it offended their pride so much that they went into a murderous rage. A nice speaker, who goes out of his way to please his audience, never says anything like that.

## Responsibility

Many situations in life require cooperation. Responsibility is the virtue that determines the appropriate burden a person chooses to carry. It is the Aristotelian sweet spot between the deficiency of irresponsibility (freeloading) and the excess of carrying the whole world on our shoulders. St. Paul reminds us: "For each man will have to bear his own load" (Galatians 6:5). The following passage specifies that Christian responsibility means to utilize our gifts for the benefit of others:

> *Having gifts that differ according to the grace given to us, let us use them: if prophecy, in proportion to our faith; if service, in our serving; he who teaches, in his teaching; he who exhorts, in his exhortation; he who contributes, in liberality; he who gives aid, with zeal; he who does acts of mercy, with cheerfulness. (Rom 12:6-8)*

It is particularly important to be responsible towards the members of one's family: "If any one does not provide for his relatives, and especially for his own family, he has disowned the faith and is worse than an unbeliever" (1 Tim 5:8).

For those who tend to an excess, that is they carry too much on their shoulders, Jesus offers the following advice: "Come to me, all who labor and are heavy laden, and I will give you rest. Take my yoke upon you, and learn from me; for I am gentle and lowly in heart, and you will find rest for your souls. For my yoke is easy, and my burden is light" (Mt 11:28-30).

## Industriousness

Industrious people use their time fruitfully and also work energetically. St. Paul gives an example of industriousness. Besides spreading the Gospel to the Gentiles, travelling all over the Mediterranean and writing epistles that we still read today, he found the time and energy to support himself through manual work in order to avoid burdening his hosts:

> *For you yourselves know how you ought to imitate us; we were not idle when we were with you, we did not eat any one's bread without paying, but with toil and labor we worked night and day, that we might not burden any of you. It was not because we have not that right, but to give you in our conduct an example to imitate. For even when we were with you, we gave you this command: If any one will not work, let him not eat. For we hear that some of you are living in idleness, mere busybodies, not doing any work. Now such persons we command and exhort in the Lord Jesus Christ to do their work in quietness and to earn their own living. Brethren, do not be weary in well-doing. (2 Thess 3:7-13)*

Industriousness is an Aristotelian balance between the deficiency of *idleness* (*laziness*) and the excess of *workaholism*. Workaholics succumb to the excess, fuss about every conceivable detail and do not stop to rest, think, pray or learn. Jesus rebuked Martha for this vice in the following New Testament passage:

> *Now as they went on their way, he entered a village; and a woman named Martha received him into her house. And she had a sister called Mary, who sat at the Lord's feet and listened to his teaching. But Martha was distracted with much serving; and she went to him and said, "Lord, do you not care that my sister has left me to serve alone? Tell her then to help me." But the Lord answered her, "Martha, Martha, you are anxious and troubled about many things; one thing is needful. Mary has chosen the good portion, which shall not be taken away from her. (Lk 10:38-42)*

## Ambition

Sometimes we have to step out of our comfort zone; otherwise our comfort zone becomes a prison that will limit what we can do and can stop us from reaching the Kingdom of God. Ambition is an ability to do daring things. It is the Aristotelian sweet spot between a deficiency of sloth where a person misses promising opportunities, and excess of folly, that is, attempts to do projects that obviously have no chance of success.

The current culture celebrates ambition and lionizes entrepreneurs who develop new technologies or products that make people's lives better or boosts the economy. Canonized saints of the Catholic Church are similar types of heroes. They discovered new spiritual horizons, started new religious institutions or embarked on daring missions to evangelize pagan countries. They were ambitious in spiritual matters.

Ambition is a virtue that is necessary in order to reach the Kingdom of God. An example of a tragic lack of ambition is in the parable of the talents:

> For it will be as when a man going on a journey called his servants and entrusted to them his property; to one he gave five talents, to another two, to another one, to each according to his ability. Then he went away. He who had received the five talents went at once and traded with them; and he made five talents more. So also, he who had the two talents made two talents more. But he who had received the one talent went and dug in the ground and hid his master's money.
>
> Now after a long time the master of those servants came and settled accounts with them. And he who had received the five talents came forward, bringing five talents more, saying, 'Master, you delivered to me five talents; here I have made five talents more.' His master said to him, 'Well done, good and faithful servant; you have been faithful over a little, I will set you over much; enter into the joy of your master.' And he also who had the two talents came forward, saying, 'Master, you delivered to me two

*talents; here I have made two talents more.' His master said to him, 'Well done, good and faithful servant; you have been faithful over a little, I will set you over much; enter into the joy of your master.'*

*He also who had received the one talent came forward, saying, 'Master, I knew you to be a hard man, reaping where you did not sow, and gathering where you did not winnow; so I was afraid, and I went and hid your talent in the ground. Here you have what is yours.' But his master answered him, 'You wicked and slothful servant! You knew that I reap where I have not sowed, and gather where I have not winnowed? Then you ought to have invested my money with the bankers, and at my coming I should have received what was my own with interest. So take the talent from him, and give it to him who has the ten talents. For to every one who has will more be given, and he will have abundance; but from him who has not, even what he has will be taken away. And cast the worthless servant into the outer darkness; there men will weep and gnash their teeth." (Mt 25:14-30)*

The talents of this parable are an analogy for blessings that we receive, both natural and supernatural. They are seen in this parable a loan from God, and God expects a "profit" in our utilizing his gifts. A failure to deliver this profit will cost us the Kingdom of God.

## Gratitude

There are many good things that we have received without merit of our own. Gratitude is the proper response to these gifts. Gratitude is also referred to as "thankfulness" or "appreciation."

Aristotelian analysis places gratitude between two extremes: *Ingratitude* is the deficiency where a person does not acknowledge the generosity that has been received. The reason is pride. Proud persons are not capable of gratitude because they assume that all good things are due to them. The other extreme is a misplaced gratitude where an abused person uses flimsy excuses to show false gratitude towards an abuser. Psychological literature studies this kind of behavior and calls it "traumatic bonding."

The New Testament contains many passages that emphasize the importance of gratitude: "Give thanks in all circumstances; for this is the will of God in Christ Jesus for you" (1 Thess 5:18; see also Eph 1:16, Acts 24:3). The following Gospel story illustrates both gratitude and ingratitude:

> *On the way to Jerusalem he was passing along between Samaria and Galilee. And as he entered a village, he was met by ten lepers, who stood at a distance and lifted up their voices and said, "Jesus, Master, have mercy on us." When he saw them he said to them, "Go and show yourselves to the priests." And as they went they were cleansed. Then one of them, when he saw that he was healed, turned back, praising God with a loud voice; and he fell on his face at Jesus' feet, giving him thanks. Now he was a Samaritan. Then said Jesus, "Were not ten cleansed? Where are the nine? Was no one found to return and give praise to God except this foreigner?" And he said to him, "Rise and go your way; your faith has made you well. (Lk 17:11-19)*

## Forgiveness

In our past, we have experienced injustices. It is painful and sometimes immobilizing to dwell on these wounds. Forgiveness heals these injuries and frees us to pursue our big goals. Forgiveness is closely related to merciful justice. The difference is that merciful justice is an act of the powerful, while forgiveness is an act of a victim. Sometimes, both overlap as in the parable of the prodigal son, which is also a parable about forgiveness.

Aristotelian analysis places forgiveness between two extremes. The deficiency is *unforgiveness*, where victims endlessly brood over past wrongs, consider their lives irretrievably damaged, and, if opportunity allows, seek revenge. The excess is to pretend that either the past injustice never happened, or the case is closed prematurely, before any restitution, or at least repentance and reconciliation, takes place.

Compared to these two extremes, a forgiving person forgoes retribution, brings the reaction to a close and figures out how to continue in the world damaged by the wrong. In the parable of prodigal son, the forgiving (and merciful) father forgoes retribution because of the repentance shown by the prodigal son.

Some ethicists confuse forgiveness with its excess. They argue that for forgiveness to be complete, negative emotions that linger after the offense must be suppressed. As with other acts, it matters what we do and not how we feel. Sometimes ethicists require that the offense must be forgotten ("forgive and forget"), which is also excess and may be impossible. The forgiving father of the parable of the prodigal son certainly does not forget the prodigal son's offense, but talks about it with the older son (Lk 15:32).

True forgiveness is a fundamental virtue:

> *Then Peter came up and said to him, 'Lord, how often shall my brother sin against me, and I forgive him? As many as seven times?' Jesus said to him, 'I do not say to you seven times, but seventy times seven.' (Mt 18:21-22)*

Jesus uses the expression "seventy times seven" to convey "always."

Rebuking the sinner may be required in case of serious offenses, especially when we are in a position to do so. This is a big contrast with the current prevailing morality that requires false "tolerance" and abhors any rebuke. Jesus describes the whole process:

> *If your brother sins against you, go and tell him his fault, between you and him alone. If he listens to you, you have gained your brother. But if he does not listen, take one or two others along with you, that every word may be confirmed by the evidence of two or three witnesses. If he refuses to listen to them, tell it to the church; and if he refuses to listen even to the church, let him be to you as a Gentile and a tax collector. (Mt 18:15-17)*

A streamlined process recommends the following: "Take heed to yourselves; if your brother sins, rebuke him, and if he repents, forgive him"

(Lk 17:3). The rebuke may, like other virtues, require good judgment and fortitude.

> ▪ **The Power of Forgiving**
>
> Psychologists say that forgiveness is a very important virtue for psychological health because carrying the load of past injuries is a heavy psychological burden. Without forgiveness, small infractions escalate and poison our relationships. However, forgiveness is not for the faint-hearted. As Mahatma Gandhi observed, "The weak can never forgive; forgiveness is an attribute of the strong."

## Other Virtues Briefly Mentioned in the New Testament

The list of virtues explicitly presented in this book seems to be long, but it is still incomplete. That's not surprising. Just imagine the number of all identifiable skills and attitudes that you need to reach other big goals.

Careful study of the New Testament reveals that additional virtues can be identified. They are often variations of the virtues that were mentioned previously. But in some situation, they play a very distinct role. Examples are thriftiness (Jn 6:12-13), magnanimity (Jn 12:3-8), cheerfulness (Phil 4:4), zeal (Rom 12:11), effort (Mt 21:28-31), flexibility (Lk 18:35-43), attention to likely consequences of permissible acts which is not to be confused with consequentialism (Lk 14:28-29).

# Frequently Used Citations

CCC: *Catechism of the Catholic Church.* (1997).
Source: http://www.vatican.va/archive/ENG0015/_INDEX.HTM
(3/19/2016)

VS: John Paul, II (1993). *Veritatis Splendor (The Splendor of Truth),*
http://w2.vatican.va/content/john-paul-ii/en/encyclicals/documents/
hf_jp-ii_enc_06081993_veritatis-splendor.html (3/19/2016)

Biblical abbreviations, Mt, Mk, Lk, Jn, etc.: *Holy Bible, Revised
Standard Version – Catholic Edition (RSV-CE)*

# Scriptural Index

# Scriptural Index

# *Index*

# Index

# Index